AYOADE ON AYOADE

A Cinematic Odyssey

Richard Ayoade is a filmmaker, writer and amateur dentist. He lives in London with his wife, her wife and their two husbands. They have children.

For his cinema, Ayoade has won no major awards.* He has also won no minor awards. He has, however, watched several award shows and especially enjoys seeing other people receive awards. Good for them, he thinks to himself in his small house that he doesn't own. He hopes they manage to find meaning. Genuinely. Because it's a tough business. Especially on the way down. And that's worth remembering. No matter how many awards you may or may not have. How good a friend have you been? What's the award for that? Who's holding *that* award ceremony? Where are the cameras then? How good a husband are you to your wife? Or to her wife? Or to their husbands? How good a father are you to your unspecified number of children?

When he's not indulging his passion for rhetorical questions or boating knots,** Ayoade enjoys receiving Google Alerts.

* For Ayoade's advice on how best to receive an award, consult his article in the Appendix (p. 211). Also, please know that I'm *relying* on you to be diligent about this. The whole flow of this work requires your co-operation, and that means going to the Appendix as and when I tell you. I don't know who you are – I now accept that there's probably not an effective way of vetting readers as to their suitability – but please show some basic humanity and fulfil YOUR obligations just as I will fulfil MY obligations to YOU. I don't need an Ideal Reader; I just need an Okay One. Deal?
** Intrigued? Check out Ayoade's classic manuals *So You Think You Know Knots?*, *How's About Another Fifty Knots?*, *Not Fifty More Knots!*, *A Further Fifty Equally Important Knots*, and the collected omnibus edition *I Think Knot*.

AYOADE ON AYOADE: A CINEMATIC ODYSSEY

ff

FABER & FABER

First published in the UK in 2014
by Faber & Faber limited
Bloomsbury House
74–77 Great Russell Street
London WC1B 3DA

Typeset by Ian Bahrami
Printed in the UK by CPI Group (UK) Ltd, Croydon CR0 4YY

Lyrics from 'Nothing's Gonna Stop Us Now', written by Albert Hammond and
Diane Warren and performed by Starship, are reproduced with kind permission
of Universal Music Publishing Group and Hornall Brothers Music Ltd

The right of Richard Ayoade to be identified as author
of this work has been asserted in accordance with Section 77 of the
Copyright, Designs and Patents Act

A CIP record for this book
is available from the British Library

ISBN 978-0-571-31652-6

FSC
www.fsc.org
MIX
Paper from
responsible sources
FSC® C101712

4 6 8 10 9 7 5

AYOADE
ON
AYOADE:*
A DEKALOG
IN DUOLOGUE**

* A brief note about the title: *Ayoade on Ayoade* is not, as some people have claimed, an exhortation to stack any extant Ayoades on top of one another. The herding and/or unethical, vertical storage of Ayoades is a civil offence. Although they appear insignificant and malignant, like mosquitoes or head lice, Ayoades are capable of experiencing basic emotions such as shame and fear. If you encounter one, especially in confined spaces like Costa Coffee, gently encourage him away from you with a rolled-up newspaper.

** Let me surpass the clarity of crystal: I'm flat-out opposed to having a subtitle at all. *Especially for this book.* It would be like appending 'How This One Goddam Kid Couldn't Even Apply Himself for Chrissakes' to *The Catcher in the Rye*. But we have one. And this unsolicited saddle is: 'A Cinematic Odyssey'.

The Marketing Team, whose every breath increases my suspicion they're the cast of a spoof, hidden-camera reality show, remain *convinced* that the only way to make you, the Great Unshowered, buy this book is with some kind of supplementary plea. Well, given that no one can understand marketing and therefore no one can refute its claims to veracity, all I could do was give these Category One Fucknuts my white stick and shades.

My eternally compliant manager (now disgraced snowboard instructor) Konnor Kaye suggested 'An Artist in Dialogue with Himself', but that merely evoked the image of some muse-less vagabond muttering to himself on public transport, while his other submission, 'Inside Ayoade', was ripe for bovine misappropriation. I gathered my wits and offered up 'The Furious Quandaries of an Auteur Didact', which I thought at least gave a foretaste of the (*contd*) linguistic dexterity the reader would encounter between these pages. But the M.T. dismissed it as 'torturously laboured'. Which could serve as a subtitle for my dealings with *them*: yahoo youths more interested in the stickers *on* the book than the riches *within* the book.

In the dueness of course, it will become apparent exactly why *Ayoade on Ayoade* is the only moniker that matters, but if you *must* have a subtitle in mind (and because of *them*, you *do*) and seeing you're on *my* goddam turf (the contents) rather than theirs (the cover), I'm prepared (with no small smattering of pique) to settle for (see previous page).

Prologu(e)mbryo

Fade in.

INT. AN APARTMENT. SOMEWHERE. SOMETIME.
SOMEHOW.

My heart can't keep rhythm. My legs are copper flex.
My mouth is left-out milk. I haven't slept. Well, I haven't
slept much. If I'd never slept, I'd be in talks with the
army. It's 3 a.m. The Hour of the Wolf.* I'm about to
meet Ayoade.

I've followed Ayoade my whole life. I am his shadow. I
am the tail between his legs.

I feel I know him like the back of my hand.** So why
am I this nervous? And to whom am I addressing this
question? No one can hear me. Idiot.

I crawl towards the bathroom, before deciding to stand

---

* I read somewhere that you should never start a book with weather
or the time. I'm worried that this is therefore bad writing. I'm worried that declaring this worry rather than redrafting is cowardly. I'm
worried you're angry with me for dragging you *down here* rather
than letting you continue *up there*. I'm worried whether this really
works as a footnote, and whether it might have been better left as a
private matter, like a diary entry or an email to someone who still lets
me email them.
** Though, on reflection, this is an area of my body that I don't
actually know *that well*. I've never really studied my hands as such.
I'll give them an occasional glance when I'm typing or trying to prise
loose the cap of a Shakey Jake, but, generally, I try to forget that I
have hands at all.

3

up and walk. I flip the light switch and blink. I can't tell whether the light is on, so prolonged is the blink. I open my eyes and, through the salty sting of tears, I see a face reflected.

This must be a mirror.

I'm looking straight ahead, and you don't get puddles on walls. You can't do splashy steps on *walls*! I start to laugh hysterically, remembering the days when I used to try.

Then I see The Face. High cheekbones, full mouth, eyes gleaming: it's a face you can get lost in. It's the face of Ayoade.

It's also my face.

I am Ayoade.

I pass out.

Camera tracks back into the inky dark.

Fade to black.

INT. BATHROOM – A LITTLE LATER

Fade up. The camera soars away from my prone body, like an ascending spirit.

Let's leave me on the bathroom floor for a moment. Don't worry, I'll be fine. Let's just walk away. You and I need to get our bearings. Because before we take the first step of *our* particular journey, a quest that will take us deep inside Ayoade, we need to get close.

Real close.

So, as Sir Mick would say, please allow me to introduce myself* (who, who?). Let me confess my *purpose*. Because an aim ain't anythin' if it ain't true. And that's what we're after here. Some good ol' veracity.

You see, for some time I've been planning a series of extensive** interviews with Ayoade. To many he's a tallish, unfit man who can't act. To others he's a tallish, unfit man who isn't funny. To others he's not even a man. I wanted to discuss this myriad of perceptions with the tallish person himself. How did (s)he end up in film? And how long does (s)he think (s)he has before (s)he's found out?

From his failed and short-lived career as a stand-up

---

* Although, given the time pressure he must be subject to (operating at the top level of rock), I imagine he'd be more likely to make any initial introduction via an assistant.
** As opposed to an extensive series.

comedian, to his failed and short-lived career as a TV writer/director, to his failed and short-lived career as a sit-com 'actor', to his failing career as a film writer/director, he disappoints with unparalleled consistency. And yet he does get (some) work. He has made two films and is threatening a third. So there remains a mystery. And this mystery, like a notable other, calls to us in the form of a Trinity:

1. *How* does he do it?
2. *Why* does he do it?
3. *What is it* that he does?

Who is this man or woman who delights and enrages me in a ratio of roughly 1:12?* And who better to find out than me, Ayoade? Has there ever been an interview book where the interviewer was the same person as the interviewee? This could be a new literary genre! A way of rehabilitating the written word after centuries of abuse!

But before I lock antlers with the man, we must put him in a historical and (counter-)cultural context. We must also investigate the Origins of the Motion Picture, and Ayoade's part in its evolution. For a tree without a past is like a man without roots; and unless we stand in rich soil, our leaves will blow like blossom into the night. And, right now, that's the last thing we need.

So, we must ask ourselves:

Qu'est-ce que le cinéma?

Wie hat es angefangen?

Who dreamed the dream first?

We FLASHBACK to –

---

* In my *Sacra Doctrina* of Ayoade, this question falls outside the Trinity.

PART 1*

CHRONOLOGY

or

TIME(LINES): TIME(LIVES) –
AN AYOADEAN ALMANAC

or

HERETICAL HISTORICISM:
TIME IN THE CONTEXT OF AYOADE

'At the end of each journey, there must be a beginning, for where are we going, except to the centre of ourselves?'
— *Transport for London pamphlet, 2010*

---

* This book has more than one part. Don't cheat yourself out of a mystery by skipping ahead to find out how many. Just know that you have *at least* one more part to come.

Ripple dissolve in.

EXT. ABSTRACT, INFINITE SPACE – A LITTLE LATER

Blurred colours blast past us, multiple timelines snake out – iridescent, infinite, alive.

From *Citizen Kane* to *Police Academy 4: Citizens on Patrol,* from *The Godfather* to *Big Mommas: Like Father, Like Son,* cinema has always produced a Good Thing and then a Bad Thing (and the Bad Thing often contains a colon*).

But Ayoade, we contest, is *sui generis,* neither good *nor* bad. Like disease, he simply *pervades.*

So let us construct a timeline. A timeline whose apex is Ayoade. Because, for us, a chronology of cinema must fall into two main parts: pre-Ayoade (the Early Period, henceforth EP) and post-Ayoade (the New Common Era, henceforth NCE). The nexus? 1977: the year of the Sex Pistols, the year of the Jubilee and, crucially, the year of Ayoade's birth.

As the digital age finally triumphs, as it becomes more and more impossible to make a film without the partici-pation of Hugh Jackman, as we wonder if there are new

---

* For more of my thoughts on the origin of the colon, consult my paper 'Colonoscopy: A New Vision of an Old Beginning'.

9

Spiderman stories to tell, we must look back as well as forward. And sometimes we must look up, especially if warned. For in our past our future lies; but in our past *and* our future Ayoade *lives*. In this way, the story of Ayoade is not merely the story of *our* time, it is the story of *all time*.

1488

Leonardo da Vinci thinks up the idea of 'moving, projected images', but forgets to tell anyone because he's so tired.

(Trivia titbit:* in a recent and remarkable archaeological find, it was discovered that da Vinci also produced a twelve-page document that bore very close resemblance to the film *Hot Tub Time Machine*. The producers of the latter have since tried to sue his descendants.)

1818

The Perambulascope. As the name implies, this system produced a 'moving-picture' effect by the spectator running round a sequential series of images mounted inside an enormous circular drum. Said spectator would have to charge at full speed while looking at the paintings, such that 'he appear'd like some infernal crab b'seized by satanic scuttl'ry'. The fast motion would blur the images together into one. 'The Whipped Peasant', 'Giraffe in Distress' and 'The Grateful Slave' were the top attractions of the day. However, there were many fatal collisions. 'Hosing the drum' was the Georgian precursor to community service.

(Trivia titbit: women were not allowed to 'enter the

---

* Students of Ayoade will know that he is a ferocious quizzer. But even the most ardent Ayoade acolyte may not know that he also *sets* the questions for many quizzes. Completists are entreated to consult the Appendix (p. 214) for examples.

drum' as quick sideways movement was thought to hurl
them into hysteria.)

1896
The first British film is released: *Three Men in a Garden*.
Synopsis: two men stand in a garden; suddenly Man
Three joins them.

The film lasts 6.1 seconds. The studio demands a cut-
down version after test screenings flag up pacing issues.
As the scene is shot from relatively far away, it's difficult
to tell whether the appearance of Man Three engenders a
reaction of any sort in the first two men. Test audiences say
that they're unsure 'who to root for' and wonder whether
they can relate to Man Three, though they would recommend the film to a friend. Reshoots are ordered and Man
Three is re-cast. A definitive 11.7-second 'director's cut' is
released in 1899 and receives generally positive notices.

The Other Two (as they come to be known) develop
drug dependencies as a result of their newfound celebrity.
1901's *Three Men in a Park*, a hollow retread, fails to
repeat the success of its predecessor. Man Three gets his
own spin-off franchise.

1917
Early VCR machine developed in China. The technology is abandoned once it becomes apparent that there is
nowhere to rent tapes.

1968
McG is born.

1973
Terrence Malick releases *Badlands*. Little did Malick

know that he would become best remembered as the subject of a series of phenomenally successful parodic pieces.* Their author? Ayoade, taking a timely swipe at the publicity hungry auteur.

1977
Ayoade is born.** Start of NCE.

1981
Ayoade begins his famous 'card-file' system.***

1982
Ayoade publishes his first philosophical paper, *The Limits of Knowledge: A New Epistemology*. Reactions range from the muted to the hostile. Ayoade descends into the first of many Prolonged Sulks. He later publishes *The Big Sulk: How Withdrawal Can Be a Victory*.

1983
Ayoade gives up his philosophical enquiries to concentrate on jazz tap.

1984
Ayoade gives up jazz tap. Ron Howard's *Splash* is released.**** Mick Fleetwood files for bankruptcy.*****

* These are reprinted, without anyone's permission, in the Appendix (see p. 225).
** Ayoade is born twice more in 1980, making it difficult to organise birthday parties for him. Ayoadeans now hold a Festival of Giving for him between 23 May and 12 July.
*** Haul ass to the Appendix (p. 236).
**** The phrasing is unfortunate; the film remains a triumph.
***** 'How is this connected to film?' sneer the pedants. Well, Mick Fleetwood is an accomplished actor, and appears as 'Unemployed

1985

Ayoade goes on a city break to Paris with his mother, but her legs swell up from the heat and he gets coach-sick.* They contemplate scaling the Eiffel Tower but conclude it would take too long. Instead they spend the evening at a Greek restaurant with poor table service. Ayoade tastes stuffed vine leaves for the first time. He can't decide if he likes them or if they're actually quite weird-tasting and certainly not a meal as such. The experience of this ill-fated sojourn resonates in much of Ayoade's later work.

1986

The period between 1986 and 1990 is largely unaccounted for. Ayoade scholars call this period 'The Age of Mystery'. Brief and conflicting accounts surface about Ayoade challenging a group of traders near, or perhaps in, a place of worship. According to some reports, a young Ayoade loses his temper and overturns several trestle tables. His mother makes him go back and apologise, and puts it down to his being quite stressed about moving schools. After this incident he is only allowed fizzy cola bottles on very special occasions, like after a successful handstand.

1991

While Ayoade is performing a handstand, the Gulf War breaks out. No direct causal link is established, but Ayoade begins to associate the outbreak of hostilities on the international stage with fizzy cola bottles. He sinks into a deep depression and loses all interest in war, fizzy

---

Band Member' in Hawaii's first major motion-picture comedy, the aptly titled *Get a Job*.
* For the avoidance of doubt: these two incidents were unconnected.

cola bottles and his childhood dream of becoming a corporate restructuring specialist. He resolves never to perform a handstand again, not even if he's on a chat show. Not even if the host asks the audience, 'Wouldn't you like to see him do a handstand?' Not even if the audience all cheer, as in, 'Yes, we would love to see that! That's exactly the kind of thing that would make this a memorable TV moment and not just a routine promotional appearance!' No, he'd just politely decline and humorously divert the hectoring line of questioning with a self-effacing remark. Perhaps something to do with his physique – he'd have to feel it in the moment.

1992

A late rerun of the film *Mannequin* reawakens in the young Ayoade a lifelong passion for the possibilities of cinema, as well as the work and philosophy of Kim Cattrall.* He will watch *Mannequin* every day for the next twenty years. As soon as he reaches eighteen, he has the first verse from the song 'Nothing's Gonna Stop Us Now' tattooed in Sanskrit across his left thigh:

> *Let 'em say we're crazy*
> *I don't care about that*
> *Put your hand in my hand*
> *Baby*
> *Don't ever look back.*

And the chorus across his right:

> *And we can build this dream together*

* See Ayoade's paper, 'In Thrall to Cattrall: A Cinematic Servitude'.

Standing strong for ever
Nothing's gonna stop us now.

Ayoade comes to regret the tattoo, not least because it makes it look as though he is unduly optimistic about the dream-building capabilities of his legs. Also, fewer people than he'd hoped get the reference. The result? He is rarely seen in Speedos, unless it's strictly necessary for the scene.

1994
Ayoade spends the next few years trying to make sense of Britpop. This conceptual tumult leaves him exhausted and angry. Its fury embeds itself in Ayoade, never to fully recede.

1999
Ayoade attempts to raise funds for his Haddaway biopic,* but is distracted by the controversy over the Millennium Dome.**

2002
'N Sync*** go on hiatus. Despite plans to record a new album in 2003, the group will not perform again until the 2013 Grammys. Ayoade has a Prolonged Sulk, only broken by –

* Ayoade wrote an article about the stalled project. Thumb your way over to the Appendix (p. 239) should you care to acquaint yourself with the details.
** It's difficult to appreciate this now, but this was once a Very Big Deal.
*** Amazing fact: before he became an actor, Justin Timberlake was in 'N Sync.

2003
Release of *Charlie's Angels: Full Throttle*.

2004
Ayoade co-creates, co-writes and directs *Garth Marenghi's Darkplace* for Channel 4. It goes on to become the most successful television show of all time, surpassed only by 2006's *Man to Man with Dean Learner*.

2005
Rest year.

2006
MTMWDL drops.

2007
Ayoade discovers a since-closed loophole in UK tax law that allows anyone of Norwegian–Nigerian descent who's appeared in a Channel 4 sitcom 50 per cent off camera hire throughout October/November, provided principal photography takes place within a sixty-mile radius of Swansea. A sweet seed of inspiration is sown. Two years later, just before the law is repealed, he will start principal photography on *Submarine*, a Swansea-set coming-of-age film shot on discounted cameras.

2008
Ayoade realises he is thirty-one years old – only two years younger than Jesus when He died – and that he needs to pack a lot into the next twenty-four months to even begin to have the same cultural and socio-logical impact as the Son of God. With heavy heart,

Ayoade backburners his subtextual critical study of Kim Cattrall* and starts the screenplay for his debut feature, *Submarine*, adapted from the novel by Joe Dunthorne. From this point on he never looks back, even at busy junctions.**

2009

Like a lot of thirty-two-year-olds, Ayoade will turn thirty-three in a year's time, but unlike Christ (spoiler alert!), he doesn't die. It is clear to Him that He and the Messiah had taken similar but ultimately divergent paths. Ayoade resolves to make a go of things, rather than allow the mob to overwhelm Him.

Ayoade starts to shoot *Submarine*.*** He will live to at least thirty-seven.

2010

Editing on *Submarine* commences. Ayoade is quoted as saying, 'Film is a collaborative medium, but so is a profiteering psychic in Nazi-occupied France.' His editor, Sam 'The Scissors' Schiess (so called because he closely resembles a pair of scissors), prefers to work alone and insists Ayoade only communicate with him via telegram. As is his custom, Schiess starts cutting several months before Ayoade starts shooting. When shooting eventually

---

* *Op. cit.* Ayoade also starts to wonder whether he'd used 2005 wisely (esp. w/r/t time management).
** Indeed, drunk with the particular self-importance of a neophyte filmmaker, he dashes off an ill-advised letter to its young stars, Craig Roberts and Yasmin Paige. It is published in *Here Are All of the Letters That I've Written: The Collected Letters of Richard Ayoade*, and is reprinted in the Appendix (p. 242).
*** Ayoade keeps a record of his thoughts in his workbook. Fly to the Appendix (p. 244) for extracts.

gets under way, Ayoade sends him fevered missives from the set and, later, regular missives (when he recovers from his fever).

Ayoade spends the rest of the year fighting Schiess's insistence that the film would be best served by an eleven-minute running time.*

2011

Ayoade releases *Submarine* in its final ninety-seven-minute version (heavily padded out with voice-over). The Top Ten Grossing Films of the Year are *Harry Potter and the Deathly Hallows: Part 2*; *Transformers: Dark of the Moon*; *Pirates of the Caribbean: On Stranger Tides*; *The Twilight Saga: Breaking Dawn – Part 1*; *Mission: Impossible – Ghost Protocol*; *Kung Fu Panda 2*; *Fast Five*; *The Hangover Part II*; *The Smurfs*; and *Cars 2*. It is a golden year for the moving image, with many films so good that their titles require a colon *and* a dash to convey their many levels. *Submarine*, containing no punctuation in its title whatsoever, is a financial calamity. In desperate need of a box-office winner, Ayoade turns to Dostoevsky's smash-hit novella, *The Double*.**

2012

Shooting commences on *The Double*. The Police are called and filming resumes. As a thank-you, Sting is offered a cameo role, but leaves after a dispute over what kind of satchel his character would in principle carry. He is replaced by J Mascis, who doesn't care one way

* You can unearth selected extracts from Schiess's emails to Ayoade in the Appendix (p. 246).
** Ayoade's US agent, Danny DeVille, cautions strongly against this. See Appendix (p. 248) for his increasingly concerned series of emails.

or the other. In the end, the satchel-carrying scene is cut. Ayoade's US agent is diagnosed with exhaustion.

2013

The Double enters post-production, the process whereby you try to make the film again, but this time from behind.* Ayoade's director's cut of ninety-four minutes is mercilessly whittled down to a ninety-three-minute theatrical version.**

2014

The Double is released. Ayoade tries to limit his press commitments by only agreeing to release a single F.A.Q. in lieu of interviews.*** He further antagonises the media by writing An Open Letter to the Press**** and A Postcard in an Envelope to the Prime Minister.*****

Despite these provocations, *The Double* goes on to be the top-grossing film of the last twenty-five years. Press reaction is unanimous. *The Double* is both summation and transcendent accession, an exaltation of cinema to the realm of pure spirit.

Four stars.

Ayoade's place in the canon is cemented.******

---

* Again, Ayoade documents the process in his workbook (Appendix, p. 244).
** Ayoade addresses the main casualty of this devastating cut in a letter (Appendix, p. 254).
*** You know where to go (Appendix, p. 258).
**** Appendix (p. 260). I've always wondered about the concept of the open letter. I regard an open letter as a *defective* thing. Surely one of the defining features of a letter is it being *sealed*.
***** Its contents known only by the incumbent.
****** Thus protecting him from muzzle blast.

Our context codified, you and I return to the bathroom and get on with things.

We FLASH FORWARD to –

PART 2*

INTER | VIEWS

or

AN EXAMINATION OF THE SELF, BY THE SELF

* I told you.

INTERVIEW ONE

First memories; childhood; an abrupt ending

'. . . *the important thing is to plant the seed* . . .'

INT. THE SAME BATHROOM – THE PRESENT

I wake up in a dry bath. Ayoade is still here, perched on the toilet, like a bird of prey.

All my life I'd waited for this.* Finalement, our colloquium could commence.

Our Ayoadium.

My first question had to be perfect, teasing: confident like a courtesan's canoodle; cryptic like the caressing breeze of an extractor fan; daring like the delicious, voluptuous melt of a Quaver.

I stilled my trembling lips. I made a sound. This was the sound:

AYOADE** **What are your influences?**

AYOADE   Next question.

AYOADE **What are your earliest memories?**

---

* The chance to interview Ayoade, that is. Not this precise spatial configuration.
** To avoid confusion: anything that I, Ayoade, say will be in bold; anything that he, Ayoade, says will appear in normal type.

AYOADE   Probably being a foetus. Conception and
         the first few months are blurry, but after
         that I remember everything.

AYOADE   So, you're minus six months old?

AYOADE   Minus six or seven months old, yes.

**AYOADE   And what were your memories of that
         time?**

AYOADE   It was pretty dark.

AYOADE   Anything else?

AYOADE   There was this swooshing sound all the
         time, and I remember feeling frustrated
         at being so restricted, both physically
         and socially. The particular womb I was
         in was quite small and not suitable for
         entertaining. It felt very much like someone
         else's space. I was literally invisible; I
         couldn't make myself heard; I was bored.
         I wanted to get out there and start making
         films.

AYOADE   Even at that stage?

AYOADE   Even then. It was either films or politics.
         But I always thought that the politics, if
         they happened, would happen later, like
         with Ron Reagan or Arnie.

AYOADE   What kind of thoughts were you having as a foetus?

AYOADE   Fairly basic thoughts, to be fair. But I had this very clear sense of biding my time – you know? I remember thinking, *Don't rush this.** Look at gestation as extended pre-production: let your skeleton harden; wait till you've got eyelids; don't get grossed out by the amniotic fluid; think of future projects.

AYOADE   It's amazing that you can remember this far back.

AYOADE   You're right. It *is* amazing. And what's even better is that I never had to rely on the testimony of my parents with regard to my Birth Story. I had my own point of view – my own way of seeing it. In fact, I remember thinking at the moment that I 'crowned', 'This could be a good scene. This could be part of a film.'**

AYOADE   That's incredible.

---

* A note on the use of italics in these interviews. Ayoade often gives some parts of his speech distinct emphasis. I've used italics to convey these because there really is a *different register* to these moments. Sometimes he'll lean forward and tap out each syllable with a soft drum brush; other times he'll speak a key phrase into a VOX AC30 amplifier on its tremolo setting to give his ordinarily flat and nasal voice a quavering, bright feel.
** Mercifully, Ayoade has yet to make this film.

AYOADE   It is, isn't it? It's literally incredible. You want to know something else that's incredible?

AYOADE   Yes, I would.

AYOADE   My mother said that I tried to cut my own umbilical cord.

AYOADE   You were that independent even then?

AYOADE   That's the implication, yes – but I don't recall that being the way it went down. I think I maybe pointed to where I wanted the cord cut, but I don't think I would've felt safe holding the scissors myself.

AYOADE   So you could say you were a natural born filmmaker?

AYOADE   Well, the doctor used tongs, so there was some intervention. And my mum was pretty dosed up. I certainly felt unnaturally sluggish for the first few days. I vowed never to do drugs in later life, unless I needed them as an emotional crutch.*

AYOADE   Can you describe to us what you were like as a baby?

---

* This directly contradicts a previous statement made by Ayoade in his 'Letter to a Young Director'. See Appendix (p. 263).

AYOADE	How many of you are there?

AYOADE	**Just me . . .?**

AYOADE	Who's 'us'?

AYOADE	**No one. I just mean –**

AYOADE	Repeat the question using the proper indirect object.

AYOADE	**Can you describe to me what you were like as a baby?**

AYOADE	Yes, I can.

AYOADE	**Will you describe to me what you were like as a baby?**

AYOADE	Yes.

There is quite a long pause

AYOADE	**When?**

AYOADE	I was about to, but you interrupted me.

AYOADE	**Apologies.**

A pause of at least seven minutes –

AYOADE	**Er . . .**

AYOADE   Can I speak? In answer to your question,
           I cried a lot – mainly for milk – but
           sometimes if I'd accidentally hit myself
           in the face – or if I'd been ignored or
           patronised – I'd scream.* I got on with
           mastering the basics – learning to contract
           my pupils – firming my stools – choosing
           a persona. I didn't have much input into
           where I lived or what I wore at that stage
           – so I tried to just let go and not micro-
           manage everything – to let my parents
           run more mundane matters, like keeping
           me alive and drawing up a meal plan.
           Meanwhile, I got on with absorbing the
           world in all its majesty and developing my
           psyche on a deeper level.

**AYOADE   Tell us about your childhood. Did it have a
           formative influence on you as an adult?**

AYOADE   Like a lot of people, I was a child before I
           became an adult – so it definitely informed
           me. I've always felt that growth is very
           important and, as a child, I had the
           wonderful opportunity to grow vertically
           as well as horizontally. Now I'm no longer

---

* A note on Ayoade's rhythm. Ayoade often speaks in fragments –
reworking a concept, chiselling at a notion, finessing a *bon mot* until
it's as *bon* as possible. It feels to me that the use of Joycean dashes is
the best way of conveying how it feels to listen to these jazzy, often
atemporal bursts. On occasion, I've smoothed out certain inconsist-
encies, redacted repetitive passages, or changed the meaning of what
was originally said.

able to grow vertically, my horizontal and lateral growth has increased greatly. I have to view Cream Eggs as a treat and not a right. I suppose as I reach senescence I'll start to shrink back down a few inches like an unattended bouncy castle.

But to get back to your notion of forming myself, I'd say that *in*forming myself is very important to me as a creative person. I'm always saying to myself, 'How's about this?' and I'll go, 'That's a really unique and interesting idea. Thanks for informing me of it.' And that feeds into formation. But sometimes I'll debate myself. I think that's very important as well. I'll be like, 'No, that isn't good enough. You need to have another idea that's even more unique,' and I'll be all, 'Back off,' and I'll be like, 'Don't tell me to back off, pindick,' and I'll come right back at me and be like, 'Don't call me pindick – that's so disrespectful and unnecessarily phallic,' and by this stage I'll be crying my eyes out – like bawling – and I'll be going, 'I'm just trying to help! That's all I ever tried to do, and you keep attacking, attacking, *attacking* me!' And I think that can be really beneficial. Just the raw honesty of these exchanges. And then I'll just get my bearings and be like, 'Maybe you need to eat.' And often it's that. It's just hunger.

This doesn't really connect in any way

– and in another way it completely does – but a key moment I remember is when I was eight years old and I went round to my classmates and told them that I was leaving school and that I'd never be coming back.

AYOADE   **And what was the reaction?**

AYOADE   They all went, 'Okay.'

AYOADE   **That's it?**

AYOADE   Yes.

AYOADE   **No one said they'd miss you?**

AYOADE   No. And it was a really *fascinating* reaction. I think they were maybe scared that if they let the emotion out, they wouldn't be able to control it any more. And – even weirder – when I said that I actually *wasn't* going to leave – that I'd made it up just to test whether they'd miss me or not – they didn't show any relief or emotion about that *either*. And that was even *more* fascinating.

So that got me very interested in issues of control and how we deal with those issues and how those issues can start in childhood if we let them become issues. And how we have to conquer those issues before they come back. Before they become reissues.

AYOADE   Or bonus tracks!

AYOADE   Sorry?

AYOADE   A lot of reissues have bonus tracks.

AYOADE   What are you talking about?

AYOADE   CDs. They'll reissue a classic album and then they'll put bonus tracks at the end. I don't know whether I like it. Sometimes you want the album to end where it ended.

AYOADE   Why are you telling me this?

AYOADE   It's just because you mentioned reissues.

AYOADE   I don't see the link between reissues and CDs. Who cares about CDs?

AYOADE   I suppose just middle-aged people like us.

AYOADE   I'm not middle-aged. I'm in the late flowering of youth. You know, it's funny: there are never any middle-aged souls. You hear about people being *young* souls, you *really* hear about people being *old* souls, but what about *middle-aged* souls?

AYOADE   What about them?

33

AYOADE   Nothing. It's just that you never hear about them.

AYOADE   And you feel that's related to your childhood?

AYOADE   No. I just – it's not – it's that no one ever talks about it.

AYOADE   Who would be talking about it?

AYOADE   I just think it's funny.

AYOADE   Like, ha ha?

AYOADE   No, like unusual. Like, hmmm . . .

AYOADE   Right . . .

AYOADE   It's an example of my informing myself of something that's incredibly interesting, and it's a thought that probably no one has ever had before.

I don't censor myself. I'll just give myself that thought, and be naked with it. Maybe it'll form the start of a film. Or a prose poem. Or an email to Steven Berkoff. Maybe I'll use it as banter if I need to talk to someone but not get close to them.

The important thing is to plant the seed. Then watch it grow. So the harvest can be rich.

34

AYOADE   I see.

AYOADE   No, you don't. What did I just say?

AYOADE   That you inform yourself?

AYOADE   Don't paraphrase me. Repeat back to me
the precise words I used.

AYOADE   I'm not sure –

AYOADE   You see? You're just like all the rest. You're
just like those stupid kids who wouldn't
admit how much they would miss me.

He is spitting with anger now.

AYOADE   I prayed every day that they'd all die, and
I hope you die too – not just eventually –
but suddenly and brutally, when you least
expect it.
        I'm going now, and I'd appreciate it if
you didn't try to follow me.

*Ayoade leaves. He protests that he's not upset and he
was joking about wanting me to die and that should
have been obvious from his tone of voice even though it
was raised and he merely wants to get some Vietnamese
street food because he's never had Vietnamese street food
before and he's curious to try some and did I want some
and he'll get me some anyway and then he'll be right
back.*

I will not see him again for two months.

I learn too late that it's best not to question Ayoade directly ... *

Fade to black ...

CODA

Seven weeks after this confrontation I receive a letter from Ayoade:

Dear ———————**

I am sorry for absconding so abruptly. I felt you were pressing your own agenda rather than listening. I am stripped to the waist and my No-No Bits are on the stone-cold palm of your hand. If I'm to be naked and honest (and I don't really feel you CAN be truly honest unless you ARE naked – which is why I'm not allowed to hold auditions by myself), I HAVE to be able to trust you. And I CAN'T TRUST YOU if you keep undermining me for NO REASON WHATSOEVER.

Anyway. I forgive you. Let's arrange a meeting soon. I'm free every day except Tuesday between 11.00 p.m. and 11.02 p.m.

---

* Ayoade is certainly a cantankerous interviewee. After he received a four-star review, Ayoade defaced the Brompton of a *Guardian* blogger, scrawling an in-depth critique of the unfortunate's life based on the testimony of said blogger's old school teachers, colleagues and ex-partners. He etched this 'life review' onto the frame of the bike using a craft knife.

** Perhaps an idiosyncrasy, but Ayoade had taken to writing my name as a series of dashes. I decided to view these as literal 'marks of affection'.

With hope for a cessation of combat,
Ayoade

PS: We've never really discussed a fee* for this, have we?

* Ayoade has gone on record as saying his only guiding artistic
principles for accepting work are 'How much, how long, and how far
from my house?'

INTERVIEW TWO

The 'cathedral of childhood'; teenage angst;
Tim Burton; being niche

'. . . this war between children and adults must end . . .'

Fade in.

EXT. A STREET – TWO MONTHS LATER

*The camera drifts along a busy London locale. Life
thrives, lives denied. Our lens finds . . .*

*Ayoade in front of a Tesco Metro, transfixed by the auto-
matic door. He is wearing three suits, the pockets full of
low-denomination coins. I offer to walk him back to his
office, a converted shipping container near the Elephant
and Castle roundabout. He demurs for a moment before
hopping into my wheelbarrow.*

*We journey in strained silence – the only sound the
squeak of wheels, the roar of traffic and the screams of
pedestrians. He does not refer to his letter. When we
arrive, I see that Ayoade has fallen asleep. This explains
why he did not refer to his letter.*

*I find his office keys in one of his man-bags, winch him
onto my shoulder and set him down over the junior-sized
rocking horse that occupies a central position in the container. When he comes to, we continue our intercourse.*

*He delivers most of his answers in a halting Spanish
accent, staring at the metal floor.*

41

AYOADE   Last time we met, we talked a little about your childhood.

AYOADE   No. You talked about my childhood. There's a difference.

AYOADE   Well . . .

AYOADE   I didn't even have a childhood. So how could I talk about it? I don't believe in children.

AYOADE   You mean, like dragons . . .?

AYOADE   I just don't believe in these cathedrals we build to childhood. I don't think cathedrals should just be for children. Adults should be allowed in as well, if only to change the font water. This war between children and adults must end.

AYOADE   What war is that?

AYOADE   Get out onto the streets, pal – you'll see it. 'The Child is the Father of the Man,' they say. Well, I don't agree: it's the wrong way round. Children should NOT be giving birth to men. Children shouldn't even be having sex! If some kid tried to make me go to school now, or join the Cubs, or make me call him Daddy, I'd punch his bloody chin in.

AYOADE   You don't regard 'The Child is the Father of the Man' as a metaphor?

AYOADE   Metaphor's the last refuge of the scoundrel.

AYOADE   Isn't that patriotism?

AYOADE   I don't think this is an issue to do with what country you're from. It's bigger than that. It's about a whole generation of kids, in estates, giving birth to fully grown men and keeping them as their slaves. And I won't put up with it. And that's why I've set up a website so that if you're a grown man being held captive, you can just log on and we use Google Maps to come find you.

AYOADE   What if you don't know where you are?

AYOADE   Then how would we find you?

AYOADE   That's what I mean.

AYOADE   That's what *I* mean.
Let's move on. I find the whole issue very upsetting.

AYOADE   Were you a keen reader as a child?

AYOADE   Absolutely. I was voracious and omnivorous. As in sometimes I would literally consume the book I was reading. That's how poor we were. There was an irony in getting *Hard Times* out of the library and feeling that there was no option but to eat it.

When I got the fine, I told the librarian, 'Put that little scanner thing on my belly and hear it ping. Because that's where the book is.' Of course, those pingers don't work on barcodes that have been partially digested, but my point stood.*

AYOADE **You were an extraordinarily creative child: writing, drawing, painting, sculpting, plumbing, etc. How did your contemporaries react?**

AYOADE I think it was very hard for them. But I was so driven in my bubble of creativity – and so mindful not to pop that bubble given how hard it is to drive a bubble in the first place – that I kind of tuned them out – like you do whenever David Beckham's giving an interview. You're aware he's there, but it's just so hard to focus on what he's

* Ayoade has long insisted that he grew up in penury. Further investigation shows that, for once, he isn't lying. For eight years he and his family lived above a kebab shop in Tower Bridge. They occupied a single four-foot-by-three-foot room. They had to sleep standing up, and would inevitably headbutt one another as soon as they lost consciousness. After a dispute with the proprietor over rent (he wanted them to pay rent; they thought they were doing him a favour by raising the ambient temperature of the property) they were moved into a heating duct. When that became unavailable due to the original tenant returning from Nigeria, they moved onto Tower Bridge itself. Days were spent dodging traffic, their only respite when the bridge closed for its periodic elevations.

saying. So I think my contemporaries will have struggled with it. They must have. Here comes this perfect kid who can do anything, as well as plumb, and what the hell are they in comparison? They're like a bunch of gutter rats.

AYOADE   **Have you always been able to plumb?**

AYOADE   I've always been able to plumb. And if you can plumb, it's very easy to get women. So there was that side as well. A sexual jealousy.

AYOADE   **Would you say you were angry as a teenager?**

AYOADE   Not especially. I think I was only really angry when I was battling injustice – and then I'd lose my temper a little bit – you know, at the sheer bloody injustice of things – but other than that kind of righteous, smiting anger that I'd have when I was protecting the underprivileged, I kept things on a pretty even keel.

AYOADE   **What injustices do you feel you tackled as a teenager?**

AYOADE   I was pretty angry about the '91 Gulf campaign. I did what I could, but I lacked a governmental mandate. Not for lack of trying, though.

45

AYOADE   **Let's change tack. How did you come up
             with the idea for *Beetlejuice*?**

AYOADE   That was Tim Burton.

AYOADE   **Oh. Do you like Tim Burton?**

AYOADE   Yeah, he's okay. I don't know if he came up
             with it or just directed it.

AYOADE   **Good . . .**

I make a note in my Emily Brontë-themed journal.

AYOADE   You're going to write that down?

AYOADE   **Yes. Is that okay?**

AYOADE   It seems an odd thing to make a note of.

AYOADE   **Don't worry. Just because I write it down
             doesn't mean it'll make it into the book.**

AYOADE   Right. It's just that I haven't seen you write
             anything else down.

AYOADE   **I think that's the first thing you've said
             that's really grabbed me.**

AYOADE   So nothing else has been worthy of record?

AYOADE   **I'm recording the conversation as well, it's
             just I'll sometimes jot down –**

AYOADE   You're recording this? Is that legal?

AYOADE   **Yes. That's fine. It's only if you're spying on someone – or if you don't have permission, or if it's Hugh Grant.**

AYOADE   Do you really think this could be a *book*?

AYOADE   **That's the plan.**

AYOADE   Because it really doesn't feel like it could be a book.*

AYOADE   **Right.**

AYOADE   It feels like there has to be more to a book than someone just saying they quite like Tim Burton, and then you writing it down.

AYOADE   **Do you 'quite like' him now, because earlier you referred to him as . . .**

I check my note . . .

AYOADE   **'Okay.'**

AYOADE   I don't know. I like him. Not everything he's done, but broadly speaking I like him. 'Okay' sounds dismissive. I really think

---

* Ayoade has long fancied himself as something of a prose stylist. Later I will attempt the first (and most likely only) in-depth critical analysis of Ayoade's prose.

he's fine. Good, in fact. I'm not sure I really want to be quoted on it. I don't feel that I've thought about it enough.

AYOADE **It sounds like you're overthinking it.**

AYOADE I'm not overthinking it. I'm being sensitive –

AYOADE **In what way sensitive? How is refusing to fully endorse Tim Burton particularly sensitive?**

AYOADE That's exactly it. I don't want to say something that could be offensive to Tim Burton.

AYOADE **Why not?**

AYOADE I just don't – I have nothing bad to say about him – and he might read this and get the wrong idea.

AYOADE **Why would Tim Burton be reading this? He's an incredibly successful and busy person. And this is going to be massively niche. And not in a Tim Burton niche way – which is also really popular. Are you crying?**

AYOADE No. I have hay fever. Can we stop now?

AYOADE **It's November.**

48

AYOADE   I'd like to stop now. I just want to rock on this horse for a while.

AYOADE   Are you upset I said you're niche?

AYOADE   No. I know I'm niche. I just want to be quiet now.
     (*muffled*) I know I'm niche.
     I'm conflicted. I'm conflicted about Tim Burton.*

Ayoade begins to stroke the mane of the rocking horse. We sit until it gets dark, which is actually only a couple of minutes more.

I say sorry five more times.

Fade to black.

* Other than Ron Howard, Ayoade has only publicly admitted to liking one director: Karl-Anders von Boten. Consult the Appendix (p. 266) for Ayoade's moving tribute to his former mentor.

49

INTERVIEW THREE

The meaning of film; being an innovator;
cinema as life; dealing with criticism;
staying authentic; a surprise revelation;
youth and anger

'. . . you name it, I can imagine it . . .'

Fade in.

The imposing edifice of a hospital, clouds glowering above. Rain lashes down. Lightning, thunder. Somewhere in the distance a wolf could be howling, but he decides not to. This particular wolf is by nature quiet and doesn't wish to blindly conform to stereotype.

Our camera cranes down through the hospital roof and into the RECEPTION AREA. Our camera signs in, gets a laminated name badge and is told to wait.

Ayoade appears to have no memory of our last meeting. Any trace of self-pity has evaporated. He seems chipper and bullish, like a bull chip. Dressed casually in space suit and spats, he sits in the ball pit of the play area, under the watchful eye of an orderly and his lawyer. It seems strange for an orderly to have a lawyer, but the orderly insists that he will not supervise Ayoade without a legal representative present.

For the majority of our discussion Ayoade plays on his own, in parallel with the other children, and seems happy to proceed at his own pace. The children do not appear

53

to enervate him, and only once is there a prolonged dispute over a toy.

AYOADE   **What does film mean for you?**

AYOADE   Different things.* Sometimes it means a thin skin or membrane. Sometimes it means the permission to dream while we're awake. Sometimes it's an invocation to *wake* from a dream. But it's crucial to note that, as an alarm system, film is not reliable. In fact, if you fall asleep while watching *Olympus Has Fallen*, you may never revive.

AYOADE   **Do you feel like an innovator?**

AYOADE   I do. And some people begrudge me for that. But I can't be bothered with begrudges. Life's too long.

AYOADE   **Do you often think about death?**

AYOADE   All the time. I'm always thinking, 'Flip, isn't death a ruddy pain?'

AYOADE   **When did you first feel compelled to capture life on film?**

---

* Although reluctant to give a *definition* as such, Ayoade expresses some of his *feelings* towards film in his celebrated essay 'Filmy Feelings'. It is reprinted in the Appendix (p. 268).

AYOADE That's a great question. Because it *was* a compelling. It was a compelling I was reluctant to shoulder – not simply because I have a stressed lower back (and the last thing I needed was to put a whole stack of compulsion on my shoulder) but because life is so multi-versal.* So I wondered whether I would be able to capture it in all its depth and complexity on celluloid. But – of course – it turns out I was more than able to and I should never have doubted myself – not even for that hour.

AYOADE **Do you regret not going to film school?**

AYOADE My only regret is that you should ask that question. I have no regrets – apart from that one. I *would* have regrets if I'd done anything regrettable. But because I haven't it would be *wrong* of me to regret *anything*. It would be a false assessment of reality. And I hate falseness in all assessments – especially with regard to reality. What is film school really? When you boil it down?

AYOADE **A school where you study and learn about film.**

AYOADE Exactly. It makes no sense. Films are things you watch when you *get out of school*. If

* I know.

55

you watch them in school, what are you going to do when you get out of school? Double maths? School should be school, and film should be film. It's the world inside out again. And besides, what *is* film?

AYOADE   **Erm –**

AYOADE   Film is life. It's not 'erm'.

AYOADE   **Right.**

AYOADE   So I'm at film school right now. Because I'm living. I'm at the goddamn academy.

AYOADE   **So you don't think there's any value in film school.**

AYOADE   There's no life in school.* It's an edifice built on chalk dust.

AYOADE   **I think they mainly use whiteboards now.**

AYOADE   Right. I don't have a good image for that.

AYOADE   **You say cinema is life. Can you imagine life without cinema?**

AYOADE   I don't want to. But obviously I can, because I'm very imaginative. You name it,

* Despite his disdain for the pedagogical, Ayoade is noted for pro-ducing semi-regular 'manifestos' on film. See Appendix (p. 274).

I can imagine it. Ask me to imagine a trout
playing tournament chess – actually, you
don't need to – I've already done it. He's
sort of sitting up somehow – moving the
pieces with his little fins. He's wearing a tie
but no other clothes –

AYOADE   **You've never imagined this before?**

AYOADE   No – I mean, maybe once – but I think the
real question is, 'Can you imagine *cinema*
without *life*?' And if so, who would buy
the tickets?

AYOADE   **Your work is so resonant, how do you keep**
from getting emotionally exhausted?

AYOADE   I can't. I'm an emotional decathlete. That's
why I always wear a tracksuit before I
start writing. Because by the end of the day
I'm sweating from the bloody emotional
exhaustion of it all. I'm wrestling with
characters, with cinematic concepts,
with the concept of cinema itself. I'm
working my core; I'm working my abs; I'm
pulling on my own heart strings like it's a
goddamn pizzicato piece.* I'm shattered.
I'm transcendent. I'm going for gold.

* Pizzicato is the playing of a stringed instrument by means of pluck-
ing rather than using the bow. The simile is clearly a laboured one,
and I had the impression that Ayoade had used the analogy in previous anecdotes, embellishing it each time. Here it reaches breaking
point (pun intended).

AYOADE   **How would you respond to people who say you're too defensive of your –**

AYOADE   That's absolute rubbish. I'm incredibly open. *Incredibly* open to criticism. It's just that I've never had a single critique that I agreed with or – in the final analysis – was right.

AYOADE   **Some people have questioned the authenticity of your films . . .**

AYOADE   I feel like questioning the authenticity of their questioning – because there's nothing inauthentic about my films – except where I've deliberately employed artifice to get to a higher aesthetic truth that in its own way is more authentic than reality. Or if the prop department has let me down. People saying that [*questioning the authenticity of Ayoade's films*] haven't watched my films enough times – you can't 'get them' after just four or five viewings – you really need to watch them over and over.

AYOADE   **How many times do you feel people need to watch your films in order to fully appreciate them?**

AYOADE   Well, I must've watched them several hundred times through editing, grading and mixing, and *I'm* still finding new things in there. *I'm* still being surprised,

challenged and delighted by things that
my subconscious has gifted me. But I think
twelve is a decent number of times before
you *might* feel confident about *starting* to
feel you'd *possibly* scratched the surface of
my oeuvre.

AYOADE   **And what if someone watches your films
multiple times and still doesn't respond?**

AYOADE   That's never happened. I think it's impossible, given the type of work I produce, for
someone not to respond to them.

AYOADE   **Has anyone, other than you, watched any
one of your films more than twice?**

AYOADE   Not to my knowledge, no.

AYOADE   **Okay, let me rephrase the question then:
what do you do when audiences don't like
your work?**

AYOADE   That's not rephrasing the question – that's
asking a different one. And the answer
to that new and frankly quite aggressive
question is that in the unlikely event that
they don't like it the audience should blame
themselves rather than the film. *They're* the
ones who are wrong. How can a *film* be
wrong? It's just a film. It can't act morally –
it's celluloid or a data file. It's not an ethical
entity. Who are you to attack a non-ethical

59

entity? It's like saying you can murder a towel rack.

AYOADE **Are you saying it's unethical for people to dislike your films?**

AYOADE I think it *is* unethical. Yes. I've worked hard and I actually know what my films mean because I've thought about it and I back myself 120 per cent* that they all make sense, and if the films sometimes don't make sense, it's because I didn't want them to make sense in those bits.

AYOADE **Right . . .**

AYOADE These audiences just show up and sit on their arses and eat chicken dippers and check their phone messages and judge, and I don't think they should even be allowed entry. I think the cinema should just take their money and tell them to go home and learn some respect. I think that my achievements have been colossal. And if people are not humble enough to admit that, they have no right having access to the work. Pay for it, fine. But you have no right to see it.

AYOADE **You don't feel people have a right to criticise.**

* A backing wastage of 20 per cent.

AYOADE   Not only do I think people have no right to
          criticise me, I also think people shouldn't
          really have rights. But that's ultimately
          for another forum. With regard to my
          cinematic corpus, it's simple: anyone who
          criticises my films doesn't understand the
          films, because had they understood the
          films they would have realised that they
          were beyond criticism.

AYOADE   You sound very passionate about this.

AYOADE   I am. I'm extremely passionate.

**AYOADE   Have you ever felt so consumed by your
          work that it's unhealthy?**

AYOADE   I don't follow. Are you talking about diet?

**AYOADE   No. I suppose you're wielding worlds in
          your mind –**

AYOADE   Yes – I am – like a mental Atlas –

AYOADE   And that must be very taxing –

AYOADE   It's incredibly taxing. Very few people
          could do it. It'd be far too taxing for
          them –

**AYOADE   Do you ever feel like you might have a
          breakdown?**

According to the tape, there is a 9m 22s silence, inter-rupted only by the sound of children's laughter.

AYOADE   'Breakdown' is a loaded term. For a few months, back in '05, I had what could be described as a 'cerebral episode', and I had to take a couple of weeks off. I'm a very creative person, so I'm always hearing voices. That comes with the gig. It's like a mixed-gender choir up there. And I think that at that particular time, towards the end of '05, I'd exceeded my quota of voices. And some of the voices that had prominence, ones that were *lead* voices for a while, were voices that had particular concerns about an interstellar race of vampiric space midges taking over the funding bodies that were refusing to bankroll some of my projects. And as a result, it became difficult to take meetings with those funding bodies because I insisted that anyone affiliated with them had to be coated with bug spray before I shook their hand. And I would go into meetings with a fly swatter. And if they said anything, I would hit them with it.*

AYOADE   **But in some ways you were probably behaving how any artist would when in the**

* Ayoade kept an exhaustive log of every meeting he attended dur-ing this period, listing the various slights he perceived. See Appendix (p. 271) for a sample extract.

company of people who wield power over them.

AYOADE   I agree. I think if Prince had done that, he wouldn't have had to spend a decade making bad albums dressed up as the symbol for pi. I'm proud of my passion, I'm proud of my vehemence and I'm proud of my breakdown. I think it was one of the most courageous things I could've done. Because what I was doing was simply literalising a very instructive metaphor about corruption within institutions. I've come to view that episode as a sort of brilliant, angry instance of performance art worthy of Shia LaBeouf. The only regrettable corollary is that I'm now uninsurable.

AYOADE   Are you still an angry young man?

AYOADE   Of course!

AYOADE   When do you become too old to be an angry young man?

AYOADE   You're never too old . . .

AYOADE   Surely there must come a point where you are too old? Otherwise the term 'young' stops having any qualifying purpose.

AYOADE   I disagree. You can be young and ninety years of age.

AYOADE   **But if we were walking in the street and you said, 'Look at the young man over there,' I might be forgiven if my eyes didn't dart to the ninety-year-old man you were actually referring to.**

AYOADE   This is semantics.

AYOADE   **In my experience people only say that when they no longer want words to possess any meaning.**

AYOADE   So what do you mean? Are you saying I'm too old?

AYOADE   **I think you're on the cusp.**

AYOADE   I think *you're* on the cusp. And I think you're being racist.

AYOADE   **How am I being racist? I'm the exact same race as you.**

AYOADE   That's what all racists say –

AYOADE   **What racist would say that?**

AYOADE   I think that's racist – I think you're completely racist to say that –

AYOADE   **Are you sure you don't mean 'wrong'?**

AYOADE   What?

| AYOADE | Are you sure that when you say 'racist', you don't mean 'wrong'? |

At this point the Orderly's Lawyer (OL) chips in.

| OL | Without prejudice to my client, I think you may mean 'wrong'. |

| AYOADE | What do you think 'racist' means? |

| AYOADE | I guess the implication that certain races have superiority over others. |

| AYOADE | Races of people? |

| AYOADE | Yes. |

| AYOADE | Not that hurdling looks funny? |

| AYOADE | No. Hurdling does look funny. |

| OL | My client also thinks hurdling looks funny. |

| AYOADE | People actually think that certain races of people are better than others? |

| AYOADE | Yes. |

| AYOADE | And you'd term that belief 'racist'? |

| AYOADE | I would. |

| AYOADE | And would you two go along with that? |

OL   I would rather not comment for myself,
            but my client is happy to endorse that
            assessment.

AYOADE   Right. I think I may have been misusing the
            word 'racist' for quite a while. I need to
            make a couple of calls.

With that, Ayoade scrambles out of the ball pit and towards the nearest payphone.

Our camera respectfully pans away.

Slow fade.

INTERVIEW FOUR

Creativity; inspiration; intuition

'. . . *the film comes to me in a vision . . .*'

Fade in.

EXT. A FIELD – DUSK

The barely-there scent of roll-on deodorant. Two men huddle for warmth amidst the barley. As night descends, they whisper secrets into the half-blue air. The cold gives their words form, making the invisible substantive.

Our camera cranes down, framing them in a top shot.

AYOADE   **Can you tell us about how you first come to a film, how it first begins to grow for you?**

AYOADE   The film comes to me in a vision saying, 'I'm a film – make me.'* At this point the film will often beckon, but I make sure that I don't go all the way to it. I'll say, 'Fine – you're a film – but let's meet halfway. You've got to come to me as well.' I'm not sure what you mean by grow, though. How could a film grow?

AYOADE   **Do your ideas always come from visions?**

* Ayoade is happy to accept commissions, though. See Appendix (p. 276) for a transcript of a short film he made for *pROject-OR* e-zine.

AYOADE   I have a hell of a lot of visions and I also
          have a hell of a lot of ideas. Let's just leave
          it at that. Let's not put visions in a 'visions'
          box and ideas in an 'ideas' box. Let's
          put them both in a box marked 'life and
          creativity colon ideas slash visions'. And
          let's make sure that box has got a hell of a
          lot of room.
              That's why scientists very rarely make
          good artists. They're too busy putting stuff
          in separate boxes, rather than one massive
          box.

AYOADE   What about Leonardo da Vinci?

AYOADE   He only did fifteen paintings. That don't
          make you an artist. That's a hobby. I had
          to do more than that for art A-level. And
          to be honest, I don't know where he stood
          on the whole box question.

**AYOADE   Have you ever borrowed ideas from
          anyone else in creating these visions?**

AYOADE   You can't borrow ideas pre-vision.
          Probably the only thing you can do is stay
          hydrated.*

AYOADE   Can anyone have visions?

---

* Proper hydration is an Ayoadean obsession, his showers rarely
lasting less than an hour. Ayoade's aim, he says, is to 'waterlog his
epidermis'. On close inspection his skin seems to *wobble*.

AYOADE   I ain't gonna stop you.

AYOADE   **And how do you feel when you're having one of these visions?**

AYOADE   I feel centred. I feel like I'm plugged into a vast energy space connected to ancestral stories: Nordic myths, Yoruba folk tales, stuff from the eighties. And, as I say, I get hot, so I need to replenish essential salts and hydrate: that's why Lucozade helps.

AYOADE   **Do you drink it before or –**

AYOADE   And after.

AYOADE   **And how much –**

AYOADE   A couple of litres.

AYOADE   **In total?**

AYOADE   Either side.

AYOADE   **So maybe four litres?**

AYOADE   Four or five litres. Yes. Sometimes six.

AYOADE   **That's quite a lot of sugar.**

AYOADE   Lucozade doesn't contain sugar. It's a medicine. For athletes.

AYOADE   I think it contains sugar.

AYOADE   I don't think it does.

AYOADE   Is it possible that these visions might be
          sugar highs?

AYOADE   You're quite a blurry man. You don't really
          look solid. Did you know that?

AYOADE   Do you sweat a lot?

AYOADE   Yes, I fucking told you. That's why I need
          the Lucozade, shithead. What's that got to
          do with anything?

AYOADE   And you're easily irritated?

AYOADE   ANYONE would be irritated by this line
          of questioning. ANYONE! How much
          sugar would you say there is in six litres?

I discreetly refer to my mini-calculator.

AYOADE   About half a kilo.

AYOADE   Right. Let's just drop it. Move on – this
          isn't of interest to anyone – this isn't
          a fucking sugar book – it's a cinema
          whatever. Jesus, I'm shaking. Do you have
          any Tizer on you?

AYOADE   Tizer?

AYOADE   It's a red drink. It's a tasty red drink . . .

Ayoade's eyes roll back; he falls unconscious. I hold him close till after dusk.

Finally, sleep claims me and we lie entwined – together, but apart in dreams.

Camera cranes up, a slow tilt through the clouds. A shooting star scores the night sky.

Fade to black.

INTERVIEW FIVE

Working with actors; collaborating;
guarding against sentiment

'. . . film is life . . .'

EXT. THE SAME FIELD – MORNING

Establishing shots of pastoral pulchritude. Dew drips from spiderwebs; delicate branches sway in the breeze.

We cut to a long-lens close-up of Ayoade over the shoulder of Ayoade. They whisper gently, as if they're the only two people in the world.

AYOADE   **How does the working process between you and an actor begin?**

AYOADE   The first thing I'll ask my actor to do is to go look at a dead body and then – immediately after – go and see a baby being born. I'll say, 'That's the cycle of life.' Our job – this *character's* job – is to deal with the bits in between.*

AYOADE   **Do you rehearse?**

AYOADE   Not really. I just have them dropped off at the morgue or with the midwife and tell

---

* Interestingly, Ayoade makes no reference to his particular (epistolary) process of *courting* actors in the first place. See Appendix (p. 281) for one such solicitation.

them to keep the cab receipt.

AYOADE   **I mean before you film?**

AYOADE   Right. Well, maybe you should pose your
questions a little more clearly. Because I
just used up some of my life giving you an
unnecessary answer. That's time in which
I wasn't being creatively daring – and I
hate that. You owe me time. And that's
a debt you can never clear. Not with the
technology that's currently available to us.
What was the question? I'm too angry to
remember.

AYOADE   **Do you rehearse with actors?**

AYOADE   I like to keep things fresh. I don't like
to rehearse. I don't like to do more than
one take. We don't rehearse life, do we?
We don't get more than one take at our
existence?

AYOADE   **I suppose not, but films are different to life,
aren't they?**

AYOADE   I've said it before: film is life.

AYOADE   **Do you think *Thor 2* is life?**

AYOADE   It's a kind of life.

AYOADE   **What about the script? Actors are saying**

lines that are prepared – it can't be as spontaneous as life, can it?

AYOADE   We all have a script that we're saying.* It's the script of conformity – of pleasing our parents – it's the script that says pay your debts off – have 2.4 children – buy more salami – don't be brilliantly brave and innovative. A script that says you will do this, that and the other, and then put bells on it. Our lives are fictions. We construct this fake reality that we're happy, when really we want to smash everybody's faces in and make them kneel down before us and beg for mercy.

AYOADE   Who's the author of these scripts?

AYOADE   We all are. And we could do a second draft if we wanted to, but we're too lazy. I did the second draft of *my script* a long time ago. Then I got on with the third and fourth draft. Now I'm just doing a polish and some additional dialogue. But there are people out there who barely have an outline.

AYOADE   Are there any actors that you haven't worked with so far that you'd like to work with?

* It's interesting to ponder why Ayoade is so reluctant to talk about the script. He certainly reacted with pique when an actor dared send him notes on a scenario, and 'outed' the querulous thespian's epistle on the 'net' (see Appendix p. 283).

AYOADE   Yes. But a lot of them are dead now.

AYOADE   I guess I meant living actors.

AYOADE   What about them?

AYOADE   Do you like actors that are living?

AYOADE   Of course. If they're not living, I can't work with them. That's in the contract.

AYOADE   Sorry, I guess I'm trying to ask, what living actors do you like?

AYOADE   Can you stop mumbling?

AYOADE   WHAT LIVING ACTORS DO YOU LIKE?

AYOADE   If you ever shout at me again, I'll take your head clean off.

AYOADE   What living actors do you like?

AYOADE   I can't hear what you're saying: you're mumbling again. Pick a level.

There's a tense pause.

We're two prize bulls, heads lowered, circling one another.

Why won't Ayoade speak about any living actors? Is it because he has 'acted' himself? Is he jealous of people who can act? Does he equate acting with a kind of

death? I change the subject, and attempt to guess at a
suitable volume.

The stakes are high: I knew Ayoade could be volatile, but
was he violent? I didn't want to find out, unless it was by
reading a report of his violence impacting on someone
else who I didn't like and who essentially deserved it, not
that people 'deserve' it as such, but there was this one kid
who punched me right on the nose for no reason whatso-
ever when I was at school and I never got him back. I
just spat blood into the snow and looked shocked and
tried not to shake, and there's not a day goes by that I
wouldn't like to punch him right back in the mouth and
watch his ugly lips swell.

AYOADE **Your work is very unsentimental.**

AYOADE I'll take that as a compliment.

AYOADE **Even though it was a criticism?**

AYOADE Yes.

AYOADE **How do you guard against sentiment?**

AYOADE I actually employ guards to do that.

AYOADE **You outsource.**

AYOADE I outsource that, yes.

AYOADE **Related to that, what do your collaborators**
bring to the table?

81

AYOADE   I'd rather not dwell on their contributions. And I'd rather not discuss what goes on at the table. My table is a very private and sacred place. It's where I eat; it's where I do my VAT returns; it's where I arm-wrestle my wife. It's a surface bestrewn with memories. Also – as a tip for the future – saying 'related to that' doesn't mean that the two things you've said actually are related. I felt that that was an awkward segue.

AYOADE   Do you feel your work is easy to label?

AYOADE   Not at all. That's why people try to label it. They can't pin it down, so they want to put a label on it. I think people who label should *themselves* be labelled. They should be labelled, as labellers, with a little label. And then someone should put a pin in *them*. I don't like being labelled or pinned. I won't allow it.

     Do you like being labelled?

AYOADE   I don't think so.

AYOADE   Do you want to put a label on this?

Ayoade leans over and gently kisses me on the cheek. Our eyes meet. The kiss becomes full, mouth-based, probing and deep. We end up making love.

When I wake up, Ayoade's gone.

I have wet myself. My mouth is swollen. My lips are ugly.

I search my holdall for fresh dungarees. I feel cheated and used. I have betrayed myself and my subject.

I am too sad for tears. I am too sad even for brunch.

Whither now?

Slow fade to black.

INTERVIEW SIX

Politics; identity; misogyny

'. . . *why are we putting things on pins . . .?*'

Fade in.

EXT. BUSY LONDON STREETS – LUNCHTIME

Time-lapse footage: a blur of pedestrians (note: has this ever been done before?).

Quick Steadicam push into –

A buffet-style eatery. Thunder, lightning.

A £5-a-head all-you-can-eat Chinese restaurant in Soho. Ayoade fills a large bowl with rough chunks of onion and sits down. I choose not to eat, much to the bemusement of the management (who view my decision as a direct challenge to their raison d'être *or 存在的理由).*

I feel both spiritually and actually bruised from my last encounter with Ayoade. My questions have a harder edge to them. I'm determined not to let my guard down again.

AYOADE   **Do you see yourself as a political filmmaker?**

AYOADE   Everything I do is political. When I eat, it's political; when I sleep, it's political; when I make love, I do so in a politically engaged way.

AYOADE   **How does that work?**

AYOADE   The exact details are between me and my co-respondent, but I might whisper something about nation-building during foreplay. It would depend what had been on Radio 5 Live that morning. If memory serves, I believe I made some scathing comments about the euro just before I touched your underside.

AYOADE   **I read somewhere that you regard your Jewish identity as being important to you . . .**

AYOADE   It's very important. It's foundational.

AYOADE   **And yet you're not Jewish.**

AYOADE   No.

AYOADE   **And you don't find that problematic?**

AYOADE   Not at all. I don't think whether I'm Jewish or not is really relevant to my Jewish identity.

AYOADE   **Would you call yourself a practising Jew?**

AYOADE   I used to play guitar, but I don't really have the time any more. I still have it somewhere. I'm pretty tasty, actually.

AYOADE **I suppose I'm asking whether you see yourself as Jewish?**

AYOADE I see myself as a man or woman who could or could not be Jewish. It so happens that I'm not – technically or actually – Jewish, and nor are any of my relatives – but to me, focusing on that part of it – the whether-I'm-Jewish part – is very much going down the path of self-labelling – and I thought we had made a pact in that field to disregard labels for all time and just be utterly free and in the moment.

I want to live *my* life in a way that's consistent with *my* beliefs, be they Jewish or non-Jewish. I'm not too sure what Jewish belief actually entails – but there's probably *some* overlap with my beliefs. I think if my life and work is about anything, it's about acknowledging the universality of *all* peoples. So that's why I get angry when someone tries to separate me from humanity.

AYOADE **I wasn't trying to separate you from humanity.**

AYOADE Well, it felt like you were.

AYOADE **Could you pinpoint a consistent ideology in your work?**

89

AYOADE   I wouldn't put anything on a pin –
especially not on its point. Why are we
putting things on *pins* all of a sudden?
Haven't we been through this? Let's keep
away from pins. I'd say *that* is definitely
against my ideology. Let's leave it to the
critics and women to skewer things.

AYOADE   **That's interesting that you should mention
women.**

AYOADE   Why? Are women a particular interest of
yours?

AYOADE   **How do you react to charges of
misogyny?**

AYOADE   I think it's ironic that the only people who
accuse me of misogyny are bloody women.
I'll say no more than that. Except that it
doesn't come as a surprise, and that it's
bloody typical.

AYOADE   **I've just accused you of misogyny as well,
though.**

AYOADE   My point exactly.

AYOADE   **And I'm a man.**

AYOADE   Well, you're acting like a bloody woman.*

---

* Is it apposite to mention that in *Big Julian*, Ayoade's Pinteresque

AYOADE   **It's interesting that you keep saying 'bloody' in relation to women.**

AYOADE   Is it?

AYOADE   **Do you think that you're frightened of menstruation?**

AYOADE   Please! I'm trying to eat a bowl of onion! I did have a frightening episode myself once, after I'd had a beetroot salad.

AYOADE   **You've never made a piece of work from a woman's point of view. Why is that?**

AYOADE   The same reason I piss standing up.

AYOADE   **You don't think a man can write from a woman's point of view?**

AYOADE   No, I just feel more comfortable that way. Why would I write from a woman's point of view? I get women's points of view all day – 'Why are you staring at me like that? Why are you so cold? Have you ever *met* a woman before? Seriously, what's the matter with you?' Writing's an opportunity for me to get away from all that and create a world in which women view me positively: the ones who support me are rewarded,

---

short, the only unnamed characters are TINY BUTLER and WOMAN? See Appendix (p. 285).

91

and the ones who don't are definitively and objectively proved to be wrong.

He catches the eye of a beautiful woman at an adjacent table.

AYOADE   Hey, darling. You don't mind the taste of onion, do you?

His eyes averted, I take my leave, and his bowl of onion.

I cannot take this brute a moment longer.

Snap to black.

The sound of distant thunder.

INTERVIEW SEVEN

Truth and fiction; Fellini; Ron Howard;
what's in a name?

'. . . everything that's ever been said about me is a lie . . .'

Fade in.

INT./EXT. LOCATION UNDISCLOSED – DAY?

It takes me several months to arrange another intervista *with Ayoade. He had expected me to pick up the tab for our last meal, felt very insulted by my sudden departure, and would only agree to meet at an undisclosed location.*

It takes me several more months to persuade him to reveal the location of the undisclosed location so that I could type it into MapQuest.

AYOADE   **How truthful have you been during these interviews?**

AYOADE   I haven't told you a single thing that's true, and I never will.

AYOADE   **I have a quote here that says, 'Everything that's ever been said about me is a lie.'**

AYOADE   Yes.

AYOADE   **Would that include things that you have said about yourself?**

95

AYOADE   Absolutely. In fact, when I said, 'Everything that's ever been said about me is a lie,' I was probably lying.

AYOADE   Were you?

AYOADE   If I'm a liar, what does it matter what I said?

AYOADE   Well, I'd know the opposite of what you'd just said would be true.

AYOADE   You assume that I know what's true.

AYOADE   Or that you know what a lie is?

AYOADE   I know what a lie is. I'm not a moron.

AYOADE   Why do interviews?

AYOADE   Because they're there.

AYOADE   How do you mean?

AYOADE   I'm not sure. I think I might've said that before I'd thought about it.

AYOADE   Right.

AYOADE   I feel it's better not to worry about what's true and what's false. Everything's fiction. And fiction is neither true nor false. It is merely good or bad.

AYOADE What about non-fiction?

AYOADE I guess that's the one exception.

AYOADE Does it bother you that the quote I read out wasn't even a quote that you'd given?

AYOADE Not at all.

AYOADE It's actually a quote by Fellini.

AYOADE Who?

AYOADE He's a director.

AYOADE Good for him.

AYOADE He's dead now.

AYOADE Don't blame me.

AYOADE Are you interested in the greats of cinema?

AYOADE I like Ron Howard.*

AYOADE Anyone else?

---

* For further evidence of Ayoade's devotion, readers are encouraged to consult his two collections of essays on Howard's early work (*Ron Howard: The Semiotics of 'Splash!'* and *Splashback!: The Hermeneutics of Howard*). Sadly, they are no longer in print, though they can be obtained by directly contacting Ron Howard himself, who has bought up all the remaining copies.
    Ayoade is also a fan of *Star Wars,* and wrote a giddy preview before the most recent re-release of the film. See Appendix (p. 295).

AYOADE   Fellini – is that Dutch?

AYOADE   Italian.

AYOADE   Right. Are his films in Italian?

AYOADE   Yes.

AYOADE   Right – that'll be why.

AYOADE   Why . . .?

AYOADE   No one's heard of him. That's where ABBA were smart. Always sung in English. You can't succeed on the international stage if everything you say sounds like 'pancetta'. And pancetta's not even a thing! It's bacon bits! You know who else is smart?

AYOADE   A-ha?

AYOADE   Ron Howard. He very wisely gave up acting before he became bald, and then entered a profession where not only is it okay to wear a baseball hat all the time, it's actually the norm. So it's almost like he's not really bald. Certainly not in functional terms. It's more like the centre of his head just grew a peak. So winning the Oscar must've been a night of mixed feelings for him. On the one hand, it's the highest prestige – the profoundest approbation that anyone in the world could ever hope for – but on the other, you're not allowed to wear a hat.

AYOADE   **When I think of him, I *think* of someone who is bald . . .**

AYOADE   Sure, if you Google-image Howard, you're going to get a look at his dome. But for the majority of his working day he can wear a baseball hat and no one's going to blink. If he were a lawyer, different story. To sum up: he picked the right kind of caper to get into.

    The Edge did the same. In fact, I think the only reason U2 tried to break America was so that The Edge could start wearing cowboy hats without arousing suspicion. Very smart guys. And team players. That's what makes them world-beaters. Give them a box, they won't even open it – that's how outside of it they're already thinking.

    And here's another startling fact: did you know The Edge isn't even his real name? He came up with it *himself*. I don't know if anyone else had even *thought* to have a definite article as a first name before. No one had *dared*.

    You know, that's why I can only give so much respect to The Rock, 'cos I don't think he's come out publicly and given due props to The Edge. I don't think people realise how radical The Edge is, as a name. Let's disregard, as if we ever could, the

99

fact that his first name is a definite article. His last name isn't a constant. It's a word whose very *definition* shifts. If we accept that 'edge' means outer point of something, the furthest place one can be, then we are looking at a name that exists in *relationship* to everything that's around it. I'd like you to try something for me. Call me over.

AYOADE   **Sorry?**

AYOADE   Pretend I'm The Edge and ask me to come over – I don't know – just say, 'Hey, The Edge, where are you? I want to show you something.'

AYOADE   **Hey, The Edge, where are you? I –**

AYOADE   I'm right here. You see what I did?

AYOADE   **You interrupted?**

AYOADE   You're not listening. That's why people interrupt you. No. What I did was this: by merely saying that I was here, I brought a very radical concept into our discourse. I am The Edge, yes?

AYOADE   **Right . . .**

AYOADE   I signify the outermost or furthest point of something, both literally and metaphysically . . .

AYOADE	**Sure . . .**
AYOADE	And I've said, 'I'm right here.' You see now?
AYOADE	**'The Edge is right here.'**
AYOADE	*'The Edge is right here.'* Simply by being in the room I am pushing back the very boundaries of possibility for both of us. The furthermost point that one can occupy is in this room. It's not over there. It's *here*. It's present to us.
AYOADE	**It's right here.**
AYOADE	*It's right here.*
AYOADE	**I see.**
AYOADE	It's a sudden redemptive reorientation of the now.
AYOADE	**Actually, I always wanted to ask – is Ayoade your real name?**
AYOADE	My real name is actually Chaplin, but I didn't want the inevitable association. I wanted to be an icon in my own right.
AYOADE	**So what made you choose Ayoade?**
AYOADE	I just thought Ayoade had a catchy, showbiz-y kind of feel to it. And it's easy

to remember. But, in retrospect, I feel I probably put too many vowels in there. I've said this before, but my name is a risky game of *Countdown*. But then again, what's in a name?

AYOADE   **Well –**

AYOADE   I'll tell you: everything.

AYOADE   **Ri–**

AYOADE   And nothing. Get out.

With no prelude and no explanation, Ayoade asks me to leave his speedboat. I explain that the speedboat is owned by the showroom; that I have as much right to be on the speedboat as he does; in fact, I was the one who obtained permission from the showroom to conduct the interview on the speedboat, despite their reservations that Ayoade would be detrimental in terms of brand association for them, seeing as the name Ayoade is widely considered synonymous with mediocrity and moral cowardice. He counters by saying that, unbeknownst to the manager, one of his [Ayoade's] offshore holding companies has been operating this showroom as a franchise for some years as a tax dodge,* and therefore he is perfectly

---

* Ayoade is a legendary tight-arse. The backlash against him (one that's been present since just after anyone was conscious of his existence – the doctor that delivered him penned a bitter letter of regret the next day) deepened when he made a recent appeal on a crowd-sourcing site. See Appendix (p. 298).

entitled to ask me not only to leave the speedboat, but
also the showroom. I ask if he has any documentation to
back that up. He opens his holdall and produces a roll
of microfilm; but when I look at it I only see the words,
'Next time, Riddler.' I lower the microfilm to see Ayoade
scampering towards the goods exit.

I vault over the side of the speedboat and give chase.

We smash-cut to –

INTERVIEW EIGHT

In which nothing is said

'...'

EXT. VARIOUS – DAY

Ayoade and I run side by side through a crowded area of downtown London. We run in and out of buildings, ducking under washing lines, stumbling across illegal gambling dens and upending crates of live poultry at the back of the all-you-can-eat Chinese buffet restaurant, to the fist-shaking indignation of its proprietor.

Ayoade wryly swipes a bowl of onion from the buffet and gives it to the Beautiful Woman we saw earlier.

Ayoade slips out of the door and hops onto a scooter.

Its owner, AN ETHNICALLY NON-DISTINCT COURIER WITH DREADLOCKS (20s), shouts after him. His colleague, AN ETHNICALLY NON-DISTINCT COURIER WITH A NOSE RING (30s), CHUCKLES until he sees ANOTHER MAN (ME) commandeer his bike. Now it's time for the dreadlocked courier to laugh. They both shrug their shoulders. A beat of shared humanity: easy come, easy go.

Ayoade and I weave in and out of traffic, dodging cars in a way that's exciting and damages some property but doesn't make you feel that a genuine fatality might result.

107

THEN:

A barricade across the road!

Ayoade screeches to a halt. A PRESIDENTIAL MOTORCADE is passing through. Well-wishers throng the streets. Ayoade's noble eyes dart up. He sees a lone sniper on the top of a nearby building.

WHIP PAN: the presidential car draws ever closer.

CRASH ZOOM: Ayoade's countenance lights up.

SMASH CUT: the president lowers his electric window to wave at the people outside.

P.O.V. THROUGH SNIPER'S SIGHTS: the car window coming down.

EXTREME CLOSE-UP: the Assassin's trigger finger.

STEADICAM FOLLOW: Ayoade racing up a stairwell. Me behind, unable to match his pace.

SLOW TRACK: The Assassin, picking his moment.

QUICK TILT UP: Ayoade karate-kicks the rifle out of the Assassin's hands and into the air. The gun goes off quietly (it has a silencer), killing a pigeon high up in the sky.

VARIOUS SHOTS: Ayoade and the Assassin fight hand to hand. I watch, helpless.

108

*The Assassin reaches for a blade stashed in his boot,
when –*

The pigeon falls on his head, knocking him out.

*Ayoade fires a zip line to a building on the other side of
the Thames and travels rapidly along it.*

*When he is in the middle of the river, he drops off the line
and into the SAME SPEEDBOAT THAT WAS IN THE
SHOWROOM!*

*Grace Jones hits the accelerator and they race away,
firing AKs into the air, while Ayoade PASSIONATELY
KISSES the Beautiful Woman we met earlier at the all-
you-can-eat Chinese buffet.*

*I race to the edge of the high-rise building and look at
him longingly, my locks snaking across my perspiring
forehead. Perhaps it was best that nothing was said.*

How could I have told him that I was pregnant? *

---

* To my embarrassment, what I took to be the early signs of preg-
nancy turns out to be trapped wind. On its release, mortification
and relief gust over me in equal measure. How I knew the despair of
Uncle Owen! (See earlier note referring to Ayoade's *Star Wars* piece.)

INTERVIEW NINE

Txt MSGs w/r/t genre, reviews, culture et al.

'. . . I like to span the totality of humanity . . .'

EXT. DOWNTOWN LONDON – LATER

The top of a skyscraper. Clouds darken. The camera swirls round and round as if in a vortex. The sky lets out a silent scream.* Ayoade has disappeared.

All is lost.

Then I realise I could just text him.

Do you feel your films belong to any kind of genre?

The genre of All Life on This Planet. It's the only genre I know how to work in.

Do you read reviews?

Only on Amazon.

How much research do you do?

For me, dreaming is research. And I like to research twenty-four hours a day.**

---

* Which is similar to the sky not screaming at all.
** Is he therefore saying he's always asleep? He can certainly engender narcolepsy in the listener.

Do you have any musical or literary influences?

> Music-wise: Knopfler, Kravitz, Kula Shaker. A KKK I can do business with. Book-wise: Ludlum, Archer, Crichton, King. And they don't lack for anything. As in L.A.C.K.

What do you think of other art forms? Ballet, opera, theatre?

> I like *Starlight Express*, which I guess is all three.

Do you go to museums?

> If I need a leak.

How would you like to be remembered?

> As the Queen's landlord.*

* I'm not sure I entirely get this 'quip'. Is Ayoade saying that he wishes to become so wealthy that he would be able to own all property in which the Queen currently resides? Or is he implying that he would like the Queen to move in with him? The former seems to ignore the enormous constitutional implications thrown up by having royal residences in the hands of one sole citizen. The latter displays an unusual naivety regarding the level of hospitality that he would have to provide. Also, returning to the former point, what possible situation would compel the royal family to sell? Are they allowed to put property on the market and keep the proceeds? Surely Parliament would intervene? And if they were in such dire need of money that they did (and could!) sell all their property, how would they afford the rent to move back in on a long-term basis? As the freeholder, might Ayoade look for more financially stable tenants? Would

**You've achieved so much.
What excites you?**

> Peace excites me. I excite me.
> Numerous things. I keep a wide
> span. I like to span the totality of
> humanity. I'm a spanner of totality.

Or a total spanner?

*After this last text, admittedly sent in anger at how
laboured the set-up was, there is a long period without
communication. Then, out of the blue . . .*

> Sorry. Reception in and out. Yes – 'total
> spanner' is a good way of putting it.
> Shall we meet? I'd like to wrap this up.

Cut to . . .

Ayoade be responsible for maintenance, and wouldn't this be unduly
onerous, his knowledge of plumbing notwithstanding? Would he deal
with them directly or through an agency? Etc., etc.

PART 2B*

(INTER)MISSION

or

A VIEW *WITHOUT* INTER

* Or not 2B?

EXT. THE CITY – NIGHT. BUT WHERE EXACTLY?

This is the reason I will never watch *Speed 2: Cruise Control* on a commercial television network. The breaks ruin the poetry.

But this is not so much a break as a break*down*.

Wherein we wonder what's happened up till now. Wherein we ask, 'What's it all about, Ayoade?'

Well, we're just about *here* –

Ayoade's agreed to a final interview; I have my transcripts; my quest is nearly at an end; I'm not pregnant. Everything's cool and co. Right? *Wrong*. Something *isn't* right. Something isn't right *at all* . . .

Something's *unresolved*.

Something's *dangling*. And it ain't no modifier.*

Why do I feel this sense of unease?** I can no longer blame morning sickness – my oestrogen levels have been stable for weeks – it's something deeper. Something darker. Something *dangerous*. Something that can topple dynasties: a question.

Had I met Ayoade?

Yes.

Had I *really* met Ayoade?

---

* You're welcome, grammarians. And while you're here, could you tell me whether I should be using so many commas?
** You may notice that there was a similar sentence structure to this in the Prologue. There's probably a literary term for this.

Yes.

But had I *actually met* AYOADE?

Don't tell the jury, but I'm *outta here*.

I need a beat.

The jury can go hang while you and I stagger into a blind alley, strip to our sports shorts and wrestle with metaphysics. (Don't worry, no one can see us – the alley's *blind*.)

And this, our tongues tacky with tarmac, is what we realise.

We don't know Ayoade at all!

Not one bit.

You see, what I'd beheld up till now had the *appearance* of AYOADE – his corporeal form – defined deltoids – abs like speed bumps – but it was merely an earthly (if heavenly) housing. And that house was *vide*, gutted, *brûlée*; its contents dissolved in endless, nameless rain (for this house contained a cloud). And so torrential was the downpour that I hadn't managed to scramble to shore. Instead, I'd been astride a canoe of hubris, sinking into the mud of obfuscation. And in that mud I'd lost my sight to a misconception: the illusion that I could unpeel the Ay(o)range.

I thought I could get a thumb in, gain some purchase on the flesh, but the overripe fruit had simply come apart in my hands, leaving me to guzzle at the pulp with unseemly thirst –

– mouth burned by zest –

– hands tacky to touch –

– I had to do a flannel wash.

I had some loose ends to tie up.

But as I tried to knot* them all up in a nice bow, I

---

* Oh for Ayoade's knotting knowledge!

started to wonder – whose finger was on the ribbon? Was it Ayoade's? Was it *hell*. And then it hits me like the pain of finding an expired Argos voucher. It was *my* finger.* I'd spent *all this time looking at my own finger*!

Later that morning I lop off my finger with a bolt cutter and come up with a new (re)solution: to never again confuse Ayoade and my (now severed) finger.

I had to approach Ayoade afresh. Not for the last time, I turn to Socrates for help. Perhaps by asking myself questions, by examining my own critical thinking, I might creep towards clarity. How does one find the true essence of a great artist? How do we get close to them?**

---

* Readers may remember the footnote on p. 3. It's called a foreshadowing misdirect, bitches!

** Keith Urban's perfume, Phoenix, is one of the best answers to this question that I've ever sprayed on myself. Never has a scent made me feel so emotionally *connected* to a celebrity. Whenever I wear it I feel like the New Zealand-born, Australian-raised musician and television-competition judge is wrapped around me like warm breath. And it's great-smelling breath! It's more exciting than the arrival of an intact Amazon parcel; it's better (and more affordable) than a genuine breakthrough in dance therapy; it's like a (safe) roller disco in my nose. I feel so confident when I wear it, as though a billion tiny Keith Urbans are gently whispering redemptive tales of outlaw love directly into my glands. What makes Keith Urban's Phoenix so special? Well, maybe it's Keith Urban's love and care in the selection of his ingredients. This pungent clarion call contains top notes of blackberry, cognac and suede; middle notes of musk, balsam and chocolate; and bass notes of woods, tonka bean, amber and leather. But for me, it's the smell of leather – a specific, manly leather smell I imagine to be a combination of Keith Urban's box briefcase and the decorative, salty trim of his saddle – that really sets this musk apart (with no disrespect to the tonka bean!). A lot of celebrity perfumers might have settled with just the smell of suede. But Urban's genius is to underpin it with *more* leather. Suede on top, leather underneath, and chocolate sandwiched beneath the two. It's an *almighty* scent. And yet the price *isn't* ungodly . . .

Where do you find Dostoevsky? On *Daybreak*? No (he's not mainstream enough).

Where do you find Tolstoy? On T4? No (he skews too old for their demographic).

Where do you find [insert name of female writer for balance]? On [low-rent programme that works alliteratively with her name]? No [further comment deriding said programme].

Where do you find T. S. Eliot? *The Ellen DeGeneres Show*? (No. In fact, she devoted an entire episode to a critical lambasting of *The Waste Land* in which she and Zach Braff dismissed 'The Love Song of Alfred J. Prufrock' as 'basically lame', before giving the entire audience complimentary egg-shaped panic alarms . . .)

You find these great artists . . .

. . . in the Work.

. . . in Their Words.

. . . in the Spaces Between the Words (commas, semicolons and the like).

And there, my fellow travellers, is where we next must wend.

Ayoade's Prose. I will dive, with you on my back, your pudgy arms locked fearfully beneath my swinging tits, into the misty delta of Ayoade's Writing.

By their fruits you will know them.

I ain't gonna let that orange* fall apart on us again.

---

* That orange being Ayoade.

INTERVIEW NINE AND A HALF*

(in which we talk to the text**)

'. . . it was IMPERATIVE that I took on the
challenge of glancing sideways . . .'

---

* This also corresponds to how many hours I've realised it would
ordinarily take me to fully unpack a five-hundred-word piece by
Ayoade.
** 'Because the cat that skins itself is no cat at all' – Jerry Mouse.

Naturellement, I'd watched everything Ayoade had been in, I'd seen everything he'd directed, but had I *read* him? I, like virtually everyone in this failing nation, was mercifully ignorant of the sheer volume of Ayoade's written output.

Ayoade's attempts to (self-)publish have yielded little interest, and collections of his film writings still have no monetary value in the West. Let us consider his introduction to *Compose Thyself: The Collected Columns of Richard Ayoade*.

As I review these pieces, many of which were written for the seminal periodical *Total Film* (hereafter *Total Film Magazine*) between 2009 and 2014, I am reminded of my younger self. Proud, muscular, tender if need be, often peckish. He was an unruly buck, determined to take a sideways glance at this business that Stuffed Shirts call an industry. That Young Man's duty was clear. To pastiche, parody and perturb: the three Ps that have protected our civilisation since the foundation of *The Oldie* magazine. His target? The Moving Pictures Business. No, not art removals, but Film: that magical, mythological projection of images in the dark.*

---

* Were it not for those fucking bright-green exit signs – reminding us all of the possibility that any screening could be cut short by death *and* that one's view could be temporarily obscured by cowards fleeing to the safe, smokeless air of the 'real world'.

For if that Proud Young Man did not glance askance, who would? Who would dare peer into those peripheral fields of film-related whim? Who had the courage? Who had the passion? Who, frankly, had the time? Especially for something so tiresomely specific. Everyone's so busy. It's hard enough to reply to emails. Even those sent by people you don't hate.

But I was often not busy. I had great swathes of time. I even had the time to look up the word 'swathe' and make sure I wasn't misusing it. I was drunk with time. I looked forward to bin day. I had it marked on the calendar. I got up early, put on a tie and waited for the adrenal surge. Yes, I had time and one other proud Prufrockian possession: an inexhaustible tub of guff.

Like Lady Gaga, I was 'Born to Do This Thing'. It was IMPERATIVE that I took on the challenge of glancing sideways, so that the readers of *Total Film Magazine* wouldn't have to. They could use their time for the things that were important to them: grimly ploughing through American box sets, failing their children, and betraying the Jungian injunction to raise human consciousness. They could be freed from the compulsion to critique film on the page, and instead direct their scathing comments towards their spouses. They could focus with unearned confidence on their sublimely average quests towards the quotidian, while I careered, quipping, onto the hard shoulder of inanity – the hardest shoulder of them all.

I believe everyone has been given one special gift. And while I waited in vain for mine, I wrote these columns. Each month I sat on my puce aqua bench and carefully honed five hundred words of non-topical, film-based piffle till the sweat poured from my shins and ran in rivulets back up to my neck.

I have resisted the urge to rewrite or tinker, preferring

to respect the pieces' raw, unfiltered urgency. It's up to YOU to judge what's been called 'some of the most prescient and vital film-based prose ever to appear in a monthly movie magazine'.* Also included are pieces for *The Peruvian*, *Film Flap* and *The Eye Inside*.

I humbly present them to you now. Quaff deeply or sip demurely – I entrust them to your care. The writer must recede and the reader must reign!**

That said, I hope and expect that this collection will change your life for ever.

Therefore, a warning:

Once you've finished reading, the gratitude you'll feel towards me WILL initially feel overpowering.

You WILL feel guilty to have received so much.

You WILL stand undeserving in front of the paradigm-shifting doors of perception I've placed before you.

You WILL brood on your unworthiness as my *mots justes* offer up fresh riches and insights.

But, please, DON'T.

You MUSTN'T feel bad about yourselves.

I *want* to elevate you.

These pieces are gifts.***

And while I don't wish to impose a 'reading' on my oeuvre as such, I do view these disquisitions as a commentary on what it's like to be a Man in the Western

---

* This quotation has been altered in order to better support the author's point. The original quote was, 'Richard Ayoade has also written prose.'

** It is unclear what Ayoade's intention is here. Clearly he does not advocate a reader-led free state, so the invocation to seize sovereignty seems groundless.

*** However, Ayoade (ironically and literally) could not give these columns away. Several close friends and colleagues said that they resented the thought of even lifting up the book in order to dispose of it.

World. For far too long, men have been excluded and marginalised from the creative professions, and particularly from film (in fact, I challenge the reader to think of more than two really great male directors). Our voices go unheard, our minds are belittled, our bodies ogled. I hope this book goes some way to allowing men one small step towards parity within the entertainment industry.

We must not falter. We must not fail. We have come too far to turn back now.

But enough.

I must march on.

As a husband, as a father, as a filmmaker, as a storyteller, as a cineaste, as a man.

A simple, heroic Man. Whom you MUST not thank.

This passage serves as a bridge – a tunnel (if you'll allow me *two* ways to cross the Rubicon) – deep into Ayoade. But before we set up camp inside the man, we need to do some literary detective work. You be Good Cop and get me a coffee; I'll be Bad Cop and check over the body (of work).

Thanks. I needed that. Here's what I've found out so far.

The underpinnings of Ayoade's prose, its architecture, if we are in the business of grand terms, stand on mixed foundations:

1. The pre-emptive strike. Ayoade is so terrified of criticism that he prefers to criticise himself (often mid-sentence, and in parentheses) before the reader has a chance to demur.

2. Bathos: using 'high' language to service his (frequently) low content.

3. UnNeCeSSary CAPITALisATIONS.

4. A wearisome refusal to use a comprehensible idiom, which, rather than obviating cliché, is a (not very) new and more oppressive type of cliché: the dreary attempt to be 'different'. But sometimes the city *is* a character in the film.

5. The chest-puff. But like some scrawny jackdaw frog-marching up to a mighty falcon, Ayoade's gnarl lacks gnash. We can only conclude that his braggadocio masks a more heartfelt desire to express *his* truth using the written word. Artists are often frightened folk; like baby rabbits, they know their house of hay is little protection from the hungry elk.

We have before us, then, a house built on five key points. A Pentagon. And like that institution, its purpose is self-defence. But you and I are looking to breach its walls.* We contend that within this prickly pentacle, this Ayoadean pentahedron, we can find the real man. For perhaps these walls form a pentagram, whose sides bespeak of magic portals. Or maybe they evoke *The Pentameron*, the celebrated collection of folk tales in the Neapolitan dialect by Giambattista Basile** that are supposed to be told over five days?

So this is the part of the mission where we agree on a plan. Where we work out how to crack the safe. The joint divides into two main areas, and we'll need to cover both.

* Of Ayoade. We pose no immediate threat to the USA.
** Credit for much of this passage must go to my encyclopaedia.

AYOADE ON WRITING

I. Writing Routines
II. Writing and Its Relation to the Unconscious
III. The Art of Adaptation
IV. A Writing Masterclass
V. Pause for Thought
VI. Space for Notes
VII. Scriptwriting
VIII. Rewriting
IX. Writing for Hire
X. Writing Music
XI. Pause for Thought
XII. Space for Notes

AYOADE ON ACTING

I. An Audition
II. Terms of Engagement
III. Acting the Part
IV. An Actor Asks
V. Pause for Thought
VI. Space for Notes
VII. Acting Up
VIII. Character Acting
IX. A Plum Part
X. Acting, with Sean Penn
XI. Pause for Thought
XII. Space for Notes

It is notable that Ayoade's 'acting' and 'writing' are two areas that we have hardly touched on in our interviews (which have been almost exclusively about *directing*). I always inferred from the way he spoke that Ayoade was borderline illiterate; and as one of the most ineffective actors of this or any other generation, I assumed he would seek to avoid any embarrassing mention of his thespian *divertissements*. But here you will find him thumping on into next week about composition and his mimetic method. As such, these articles serve as a road map to areas of Ayoade as yet unseen.* Where appropriate, I have added my own comments and analysis. An author's attempt at cartography, if you will.

But before you undertake this journey, allow *me* to issue a warning of my own: this is long, arduous work. Do not attempt to read these articles in one go. Take breaks. There are designated rest points for you to gather your wits and make notes.** In fact, I would recommend that you put aside no less than FIVE days to read these pieces. There are sixteen in all: that's 3.2 a day, which is pretty good going. But even that will be tougher than anything you've experienced in your reading life. I once read seven of Ayoade's articles in a row, and I was so shattered that I developed a rash on my anus.

If you feel depressed, contact a loved one. If you have no loved ones, your depression may have other causes. If the depression won't lift after a few days, I advise you to skip straight to Part 2C, in which we will conclude our business with Ayoade. Many have given up after just one of Ayoade's articles.*** There is no shame in this.

* Unless you've already read them.
** It's always a moral quandary: should one deface a book by writing your thoughts on its pages? My recommendation? Keep this as your 'reading' copy and buy another book for 'best'.
*** I hear the spleenful trill of a pedant, 'But we've already (*contd*)

Reading *any* of this material is an achievement.

We are comrades.

I'll see you on the other side of the wind.*

---

read several of Ayoade's articles. They've been *littered* about the place – disguised as footnotes. We've grimly flicked back and forth. We've *engaged*. We can do this. We're tired – yes, of course we're tired – we're *exhausted* – but we *can* do this. Don't patronise us.' To which I answer: 'Yes. You have done well. Very well. And I'm proud of you. And I want to give you an acknowledge. And a praise. But any articles you've read up till now have been employed as illustrations to a point *I* was making. You had a very clear objective going in, and you were generally back out in five hundred words or less. I was effectively holding your hand all the way through. If I had *started* by grouping Ayoade's material along purely thematic lines, and then thrown you straight at it, unsupervised, it would've been like taking the training wheels off your trike and shoving you down a hill: a mistake I have made only twice while looking after my nephew. I had to get you ready. You're my responsibility. We had to wait till it was the *right time* for your mind *and* your body to do this. And this is the right time. So just trust me. I've got you this far, haven't I?'

* I.e. p. 195.

Syntactical Insincerities:
Ayoade on Writing

I. WRITING ROUTINES

Gustave Flaubert said, 'Be regular and orderly in your life, so that you may be violent and original in your work.' But he also said, '*Madame Bovary, c'est moi*' – a clearly false and misleading statement. However, there is something to be said for routine, especially for a screen-writer as violent and original (in life and in work) as me. Here, I outline an average day in the life of Ayoade.

I wake up at 5.45 a.m. Then I go back to sleep because it's only 5.45 a.m. I'll get up again as soon as it's less early than before (which is immediately), stare for a while, close my eyes once more and try to doze for a bit. By this point I'm quite confused, so I'll climb under my bed with a laptop and start Googling myself. This can take up to four hours. Then:

09.45–11.00 a.m.: tax evasion
11.00–11.20 a.m.: biscuit break
11.20–11.30 a.m.: crying

After the final few sobs, I'll start my workout routine and eat a couple of nectarines. I've always loved nectarines – ever since I found out they were like peaches, only smooth. I like peaches, but somehow I've never trusted them. Nectarines have been the ideal solution. Sometimes I'll try and find out how much milk I can drink before feeling uncomfortable, but now I more or less know my limits, so I can just consult my notes if I forget.

12.30–12.40 p.m.: additional Googling
12.40–12.50 p.m.: return unwanted Amazon items
12.50–13.00 p.m.: order further Amazon items
13.00–13.10 p.m.: Spanish lesson

Then it's time for a Kia-Ora. It's vital to replenish the well of my unconscious, and weak, nostalgic juice drinks help.

At about 2.00 p.m. I'll spend a half-hour gurning in front of my pocket mirror to keep my acting chops supple. I only have one acting muscle, subdivided into two or three chops, and I try to look after it/them. I never know when I'll next be called on to pretend to be a fictional person, so I'm forced to maintain a constant state of vigilance. That's why I eat so much raw fish.

At 5.00 p.m. I like to make sushi but am sadly unable to, having never mastered (or indeed attempted) the craft. Therefore I eat a lot of curry, even though the term 'curry' is a displeasingly vague term that refers more to a pan-Asian phenomenon catering to particular national tastes than a specific type of cuisine.

At 6.00 p.m. each day I pause to reflect on the fact that Justin Hayward from The Moody Blues wed former model Ann Marie Guirron on 19 December 1970 and that they have one of the most stable marriages in rock, and could I use this fact in a script, but it never quite seems to sound natural.

Then I'll take a walk (or a swim if I'm in water). I make sure to wear high-stability shoes with a firm mid-sole. Buying shoes can be a daunting transaction tinged with bitterness, but I endeavour to conduct my purchases in a humane and respectful manner.

Every other day I pick up my mother from wrestling practice. She's a loving mother, and an accomplished wrestler. The wrestling studio she uses is in a secret but secure location in south Kent. In my low moments I wish she could find somewhere nearer to where I live, but she seems to like it there, and the bus ride to and fro allows me to experience what it's like to be on a bus for seven hours in a row. It's on these trips that I have some of my best ideas. For example, I had the idea to stop picking up my mum from wrestling practice, but I soon realised she'd beat the shit out of me.*

* But when does Ayoade *write*? Has he forgotten to mention it or does he just *not write*? Maybe if he stopped writing articles about his writing routines he'd find the time to *actually* write something.

II. WRITING AND ITS RELATION
TO THE UNCONSCIOUS

In order to further harness my own creativity, I now keep a dream diary (if I wish to further harness *myself*, I'll wear a bridle). As a result my sleep has become just another day at the office, except with fewer snack breaks. Herewith selected extracts from this record of reverie; my inventory of imaginata; an admittedly all-too-alliterative almanac of altered states.

Dreamt I won the Allergy Sufferer of the Year award and that Rick Moranis came out of retirement to present it, and I was so flushed with happiness that I stopped sneezing and was consequently disqualified. Then Sir Ben Kingsley told me how acting was like archery and how he had to become the arrow AND the bow and how hard that was, and I said do you think that's because you sort of *look* like an arrow? But he wasn't listening any more because he had to restring himself, and I started to wonder whether he really suffered from allergies or whether he was just there to network.

Dreamt I was trapped in an awful cycle of only being able to give the same limited 'acting' performance in everything I do, before realising I was awake and that I really am very limited as a performer, but then I remembered that I tend to have very literal dreams, so I was briefly unsure whether I was actually asleep but had just *dreamt* that I had woken up or whether I really *was* awake, before having the more dispiriting thought that it didn't really *matter* whether I was awake or asleep unless I was in charge of a vehicle or heavy machinery, in which case whatever damage I'd done was most likely already done and I was probably unconscious in some hospital about to have a botched operation and that my last-ever dream would have been exhaustingly circuitous and meta and not in a cool way like Charlie Kaufman probably dreams and then Sir Ben Kingsley had a sneezing fit and I felt bad for doubting him.

Nicolas Cage kept trying to offer me his wig and saying, 'It works, man, I'm telling you,' and doing alternately swoopy and stabby hand gestures. I said I need to scrub down this yacht or they won't give me back my bionic eye. He suggested we team up and then we were on big bikes and he was screaming and I was trying not to get sand in my empty eye socket but I didn't have goggles and now my mouth was full of sand and I thought how come Nicolas Cage manages to keep the sand out of *his* eyes and mouth?

Selected Power Naps

Dreamt I was in an alternate reality in which *Sliding Doors* had never been made. It was pretty much the same as this reality, except fewer people beefed about it ripping off Kieślowski's *Blind Chance*.

Dreamt that *The Hangover* trilogy didn't happen. The world went on.

III. THE ART OF ADAPTATION

So you've been asked to adapt a novel. Where in whoops do you start? Behold the Ten Commandments that helped me *navigate* the choppy waters of *Submarine*.*

1. As tedious as it may seem, try to read the novel rather than just skimming through the Wikipedia summary. You will have to read most (if not all!!!!) of the novel. I know: books are annoying and outdated. But stick with it because you're going to turn it into something far more important: audio-visual content that can exist on multiple platforms.

2. Screenplays tend to use bigger-sized paper than novels (see Figure 1 on p. 141). Confusing, I know! But you'll soon get used to it. Try getting your manager or legal team to enlarge the novel to A4 size before you start your adaptation. Then write 'INT' or 'EXT' at the start of the passages that you think might make a sweet piece of action in your rad film.

---

* It's unclear whether Ayoade thinks this pun works or whether it's deliberately bad. Surely the 'submarine' referred to would be *under* the water. The use of the possessive here has the unfortunate effect of implying that the 'submarine' referred to is *composed* of choppy waters. Surely 'Here are the Ten Commandments that helped me steer my *Submarine*' would be clearer and as funny (i.e. in no way funny) as Ayoade's mangled melange.

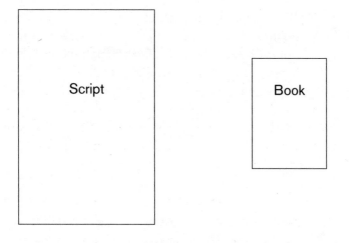

Figure 1

3. Even so-called 'short novels' are pretty long and can take several hours to read, so make sure you stay hydrated. I like to keep an isotonic sports drink handy if I'm going to be reading for any longer than forty minutes.* I'll also take regular breaks and make sure I'm wearing loose-fitting clothing.

4. Capitalise to convey urgency. E.g. Ingmar SMASHED the small ALARM CLOCK into the RIBS of the ARCHDEACON.

5. Stage directions should be brief. E.g. 'The ECUMENICAL COUNCIL DETONATED into a FLESH SHOWER' can be more economically conveyed as 'THE BISHOPS BLEW UP'.

* See earlier note on hydration (p. 70).

6. Books contain surprisingly little necessary information. A quick way to plough through an adaptation is to type out everything from the novel that's
in inverted commas. This should cover most of the
important dialogue.

7. You've taken care of structure. What about theme/
meaning and all that shit? Is there a clue on the
dust jacket or in the press release? If not, call the
author and ask him to explain himself. If he finds
that unsettling, start using threats.

8. So you're in court for threatening the author.
Deal with it. If you want to be in the film business, you'll have to become accustomed to suing,
counter-suing and defending a variety of criminal
charges.

9. So you've settled out of court for an unspecified
amount. Back to work. You need the money to
clear your expenses, so you've taken a commission
to adapt another book (a further legal case looms).

10. Return to point one.*

* So this should really be Nine Commandments, no?

IV. A WRITING MASTERCLASS

Recently I was asked to teach a masterclass in screen writing at an eminent college in north-west Norway. Its charming rector, Flaggkommandør Knut Ellefson, reassured me that although they *had* initially booked me because they thought I'd made a film *about* submarines, many of the cadets in attendance had a genuine interest in my work. And if I could make it relevant to people interested in underwater combat, so much the better.

Desperate for paid employment, I accepted. I'd been slaving for days, unwaged, on my passion project ('Yeast, A Journey' – a story about a deaf mute pastry chef sent to the Crimean War, told from the point of view of some yeast) and was struggling to get any financiers to stump up for my initial stationery costs. But although the £130 fee (not inclusive of ferry fare and cabin rental) was welcome, what really excited me was the opportunity to codify some of my insights on script writing. Over the next few weeks I hope to expand on this topic,* but for now, as an *amuse-bouche*, my edited transcripts of that now legendary lecture.

---

* Interestingly, Ayoade never does. It seems that he was able to say almost everything he had to contribute to the subject of scriptwriting in this aborted seminar.

143

AYOADE strides to the stage. Applause, then hushed expectation. After some time the microphone is located and the talk can begin.

Thanks, or should that be '*Takk skal du ha*'? You must forgive my accent – I'm Finnish!

Nothing. Some smiles.

And how about that wind-dried sheep's head? I think the smorgasbord deserves its own round of applause . . . If overfishing is wrong, I don't want to be right!

Coughs.

Anyhoo, let's get down to it, as the Dane said to the Swede.

Creaks. The scuff of harpoon on flagstone.

Okay. Let's keep it tight. My name is Richard and I'm a screenwriter. But what is a screenwriter? Am I a prophet? A sage? A healer? Or all three? That's what you're here to discover.

So, without further ado, let's right some wrongs about writing. Or, for the cynics among you, *write* some wrongs . . . Or, for the ceremonious, *rite* some wrongs . . . Sorry, that would probably have worked better if English were your first language.

At this point there's a long argument with an EXPAT which I've deleted here.

Imagine that 'Film' is a gargantuan mechanism beneath, say, the ocean. How can it find its way? It needs a periscope. And that's what the script . . . Yes? You have a question?

No, I don't know what an optronic mast is.

Giggles. Long-winded explanation of why periscopes are no longer used in the Norwegian Navy.

Well, I think the metaphor stands.

Chatter. A loss of focus. AYOADE rises up, a wild stallion on a moonlit plain protecting his mares from a wily trapper.

Okay, you sea dogs, I didn't want to do this till after the meatballs, but you leave me no choice . . .

AYOADE removes a large red box from his knapsack. Strange light emanates from it, his manly countenance illuminated with the fierce glow of wisdom.

These . . . are my secrets.

The audience breathes in as one.

Damn. I left my bike light on.

AYOADE switches off the red light. The box now appears more brownish. He takes off the lid and fishes out a stack of cue cards. The audience breathes out. The air smells of herring and hate.

Have you heard the old Hollywood joke about the starlet who's so stupid that she tries to get ahead by sleeping with a writer?

An AUDIENCE MEMBER says, 'No. What is it?'

AYOADE is forced into making a long digression about how that actually was the joke, and no, he didn't find it that funny either, but that it did make structural sense. Wearied, he presses on.

Okay, let's return to the question of what is a screen-writer. In fact, let's break down that very word, shall we? Screen. Writer. How does the notion of 'screen' mod-ify the idea of 'writer'? In fact, what is a 'screen'? Is it the computer screen onto which we peck out our lofty dreams, or the silver one onto which we project them?

A CADET in the audience tries to take his own life. FLAGGKOMMANDØR ELLEFSON quickly intercedes, insisting this is a not unusual occurrence. The days are short in Norway, and the news that A-ha were definitely not going to re-form again still hung heavy over the nation. Shaken, AYOADE continues, but changes tack somewhat.

Okay, put it this way. Why do I write? This is the ques-tion almost everyone who has ever seen my work has asked. And I have, in countless letters, text messages and prison visits, essayed a reply. I believe a writer is someone who, in some small way, tries to set the world to rights, much like a serial killer or Noel Edmonds. And, like Noel Edmonds, the writer can be a tough person to like.

The man who tried to take his life now tries to take the life of AYOADE. A long-time devotee of Edmonds, the CADET can brook this insolence no longer. Ayoade and his naval adversary tumble into an ice sculpture of the figure from Edvard Munch's The Scream. *It shatters, a seemingly more poetic end to its life than merely melt-ing. The talk is abandoned. Ayoade disgraced.*

146

V. PAUSE FOR THOUGHT

– What is Ayoade trying to achieve with these articles?

– What are the moral underpinnings (if any) at work in these articles?

– Is Ayoade's 'voice' consistent in these articles?

– Are the articles structurally consistent? If so, in what possible way?

– Are these articles structurally coherent? If so, how?

– Can you identify any repeated thematic concerns in the articles? Or are they just a mish-mash?

– Why does the last article end so abruptly? Is its lack of conclusion intentional, or just casually frustrating?

VII. SCRIPTWRITING

Script, n., the words of a film, play, broadcast or speech. *The Script*, n., an Irish pop rock band.

Every good film starts with the script. As does a bad film. A really bad film starts with The Script. Unless it's a biopic of The Script, in which case it may also end with The Script, like a mad snake eating its own tail. But no script is perfect straight away. Sometimes I'll rewrite a script up to two times to get it just right. Occasionally I'll even cut something from the first draft. The key is Discipline, Discipline, Discipline. Or, to be more concise, Discipline, Discipline.

   Herewith a sample of one week's labour (notes in bold).

MONDAY
Fade in.

'The Man Who Can't Be Moved' by The Script plays on the soundtrack.

We open on TONY'S FACE.

What do we open? And why are we on TONY'S FACE? Shouldn't we open whatever it is we're opening on DANNY'S FACE?

TUESDAY

We open on the face of DANNY O'DONOGHUE,
lead singer of The Script (30s). He's riding in a jet-black
limo, exhausted from a big sing. He sups a Guinness and
closes his twinkly Irish eyes. The camera finds him lost in
a DREAM.

Question: how does a DREAM differ from a dream? Can
you have a DrEaM? Also, can he put the Guinness in a
cup-holder? Otherwise I'll be tense all the way through
this Dream Sequence.

WEDNESDAY

We DISSOLVE to a scene of a much younger DANNY
O'DONOGHUE. He gently sings to himself as he walks
down a cobbled street in downtown Dublin. There's a
maturity to his voice, a pain eminently suited to melodic
rock. A LOVELY IRISH GIRL smiles at him.

Is this a good idea? Would mean booking TWO actors
plus a child minder. Love the character of LOVELY IRISH
GIRL, though.

THURSDAY

We cut to YOUNG DANNY (PLAYED BY THE
SAME ACTOR AS OLD DANNY) looking at a tub of
hair gel on a display stand in a TOP DUBLIN SALON.
It seems illuminated by a special light. (It does in fact
have a small light shining on it.) DANNY gazes down
at his hand. He has just one euro. ECU HAIR GEL
PRICE TAG: TWO EUROS!

I love this! How's he going to get an additional euro?!

150

FRIDAY

DANNY tacks up an ad on an Irish noticeboard:
'Musicians wanted to produce melodic rock music for TV
shows/bra ads etc.'

Possible theme unexplored so far – how can we
reconcile the idea of a loving God with the existence of
evil/The Script and, further, could our consciousness
comprehend such reconciliation even if one were
possible? But good work this week! See you Monday!*

---

* Ayoade never made this film, and its script now resides in a drawer filled with several other never-to-be-realised rock-related projects, including:

Me2: Sprightly rock musical in which a rag-tag group of ne'er-do-wells childishly insists on copying everything that the band U2 does, until the disparity in their respective resources makes this impossible. Eventually U2, making a knowing cameo appearance, allow the young acolytes the chance to open for them on tour, movingly joining them in a rousing and thematically relevant rendition of the song 'With or Without You'. Ayoade was halfway through his eighth draft when a colleague casually mentioned that he might want to seek the permission of U2.

The House of Bernarda Alba with Bananarama: the concept was to have all eighteen of the main female parts played by a member of the girl-group trio and to film the multiple roles using motion control and split screen. However, while selecting six parts each for Sara Dallin, Keren Woodward and Siobhan Fahey was relatively painless, a vicious fight broke out over who would play the part of 'various women mourners', with each member insisting that they wanted to play all of them. Things were said that could never be taken back, and the project foundered.

Tears for Bears: in which the rock band Tears for Fears exchange their tears for two bears instead of fears, invoking the wrath of several other bears, as well as causing general media confusion over how best to position the band in the marketplace, esp. w/r/t branding, etc.

VIII. REWRITING

Last year I took a brief rewrite job on the upcoming Hollywood 'bromance' *Hot Sauce II: Afterburn*. Although I was a great admirer of the original *Hot Sauce!*,* I must confess that my involvement with its sequel was motivated, in part, by financial concerns (having used the small amount of money I'd made in niche and critically lambasted 'comedy' shows to pay the interest on some of my more pressing bills). Nevertheless, I felt I'd made many vital improvements to the script.

I handed in my draft and never heard from the studio again. So it was with great surprise that I was copied in on an email proudly announcing the test results from an early screening of *HS2A*. The response had been rapturous, and I was pleased to discover that my lovingly applied grace notes were still sounding sweetly.

---

* A brief synopsis, from memory:
  Clark has just been dumped by his girlfriend, Tara, for barging in on her when she was trying to have sex with some work colleagues. Meanwhile, Clark's handsome, muscle-bound roommate Vito keeps him up all night with his amorous antics. But when Clark is fired from his job as a male nanny to a couple of uptight, gay Mexican restaurateurs with mafia connections, he decides to concentrate on his passion project: developing the ultimate spicy sauce. Something with intensity; something with flavour; and, most importantly, something with afterburn.
  After much experimentation, his bowels in disarray, he succeeds in producing the Ultimate Hot Sauce. To celebrate, Vito persuades him that they should both go out to Vito's favourite strip club. Mysteriously, all the women seem to be drawn to Clark and not Vito, as well as in no way seeming to be preoccupied by personal sadness. Indeed the hottest

Film:	*HOT SAUCE II: AFTERBURN*

Audience Reaction: *The overall audience reaction was incredible. The audience was very involved, they laughed throughout the entire movie. The audience applauded at the end and kept laughing even through the credits, which were white on black. One man said it was the best movie he'd ever seen and that he wanted to die now because he was told the movie wouldn't be out for a month and he didn't think he could stand to live that long without seeing the movie again.*

---

stripper, Misty Canyons (who, according to Vito, is 'a stuck-up tease that won't give any john any piece of anyhoo'), singles Clark out for particular attention. Misty and Clark make a date. During their truck ride back, Clark and Vito discuss the evening and conclude that the titular Hot Sauce must cause some massive boost to the production of male pheromones. A later experiment confirms this theory. Vito takes the noble decision never to try the Hot Sauce, claiming it wouldn't be fair given that he's already 'drowning in beaver, bro'. But later, after a rare moment of performance anxiety with a lapsed Lutheran, Vito consumes a whole bottle of Hot Sauce. Events escalate and, before long, the Canadian netball team is forced to withdraw from the Olympics.

Hot Sauce becomes a global sensation. Clark is making crazy money. Tara, contrite, returns to find Clark. Despite Vito's repeated warnings not to settle for 'a last meal when he could be at the buffet, bro', Clark accepts her back. Vito and Clark become estranged, Vito accidentally overdosing on Hot Sauce at an après-ski event. After a mourning montage, Clark finds out that Tara is working for the Mafia via the gay Mexican restaurateurs, and he decides to shut down all Hot Sauce production and burn the recipe, but not before having to fight for his life in several thrilling high-octane sequences that allow him to make propulsive use of his now chronic flatulence. He apologises to Misty Canyons. She is unmoved, until a timely eruption breaks the tension, and they embrace.

His assailants vanquished, he takes up a new job as head chef at a spicy-chicken and pole-dancing concession stand that he now co-owns with new wife, Misty Canyons, who, it turns out, has no sense of smell and is unaffected by pheromones.

Favorite moments:

When we first see Clark and he's masturbating in the toilet and we find out he's meant to be a teacher.

When we see Donald and he's trying to touch his balls with his fingernails painted to look like a lady's hand and then we see he's in a job interview.

When the gay guys fart in the hi-fi store.

When the fat one trips on the cake and knocks over the other cake.

When Clark and Donald make the baby look like he's rapping.

When you can almost see Donald's penis.

When they have the party and it gets out of hand.

When they kill the French guy.

When Brian is caught on the toilet by his stepson.

When they all do drugs that aren't serious enough to make you feel that it's not going to end up being fun but there are enough consequences to make it look like the film isn't totally condoning drugs even though the writers probably smoke a lot of pot and maybe do mushrooms sometimes or coke if they're tired and maybe some Valium to help them sleep.

When the old lady is wearing sunglasses in the hot tub.

154

When they do drugs with the old lady.

When the old lady takes her top off.

When Clark gets an erection in the hot tub and has to wait until he no longer has an erection.

When they're handcuffed to the horse.

When Donald goes small for a while and they don't know why.

When Clark's hair goes curly.

When they blow up the pond and the fish go everywhere and the girl's T-shirt gets wet and it's kind of sexy but also melancholy somehow.

When Brian and Clark say they'll miss one another and it looks like they might kiss and then they both say 'gay!' and then the fat one says he *is* gay and they say they're both cool with that and so is Donald eventually.

When Clark leaves his teaching job and makes a speech and the kid that caught him masturbating applauds.

IX. WRITING FOR HIRE

In which Ayoade shares an email from legendary movie mogul Irwin Chase, producer of such films as *Show Me that Chicken!* and *Ladies, Ladies, Ladies!*.

Hey,

Great to sit down with you recently. I'm still psyched about that thing you said. What was it again? I can't remember. Maybe I was texting or something. Let my assistant know if you remember it and I'll get him to tell me it or you could tell it me directly if you think that'd be better – totally up to you if you want to get me direct and feel free to ask my assistant to forward emails or whatever – your call. Anyway – here's that idea that I said I was going to send you and then didn't and now am. I think the skeleton of it's really solid – you'd just have to put flesh on it and skin and maybe some hair or whatever and possibly clothes. I don't know. Metaphors aren't really my thing. In fact they kind of make me angry.

Title: *Back to the Future*
The Concept: A man wakes up to find that his back is facing/leaning up against the future. Literally! The front half of him is in a different time continuum to the back half! He's two men! Or one man bisected vertically!

The Talent: Ashton Kutcher plays the front half (sassy – always knows what lies ahead) and Harrison Ford the back (grouchy – set in his ways, has an inexplicable ear stud) and we join them using CGI.

The Plot: They disagree on what pants to get; maybe they have a job or something. Also you could have a good scene in the tub. Maybe one prefers showers. Or maybe one digs sports more than the other or has different ideas about how to spend his time. Could be a funny scene where one of them wants to run away from the other but can't because he's joined to the other one and maybe they start hitting one another and possibly people start watching them and it could maybe be Christmas and for some reason they're in a fancy department store and they end up kicking Santa Claus or possibly a Chinese kid in the balls (doesn't have to be Chinese, but I think that could work – especially if the manager was showing some Chinese/Japanese businessman around because he had some big deal that he needed to get signed off that day). All you have to deal with is the space/time/future-y stuff so we can make sense of the title – your call – but I definitely want wormholes at some point.

Let me know what you think. Could be a lot of fun, especially if we get a love interest (when Ashton is making it with the girl, Harrison could be really pissed because he's trying to read a book or something – maybe he orders pizza! On his cellphone! While Ashton is dinking Jessica Alba, if we can get her!).

Only real barrier is that the title's been used – but maybe that's a good thing? It WAS a long time ago. In any case, people will feel like they've heard it before and be more likely to go.

Let me know ASAP and I'll rustle up the cast – maybe you can handle getting the title?

X. WRITING MUSIC

It's a well-established fact that I almost worked on Paul Thomas Anderson's *There Will Be Blood*. In the end, Danny Lewis took the role that I (graciously) declined. However, not many people know that I was also meant to write the music. PTA was a big fan of my tuba-playing in the cult, all-brass punk band The Horn-ettos and collared me after a gig. He showed me an early cut of the flick and, though the first twenty minutes were a little light on banter, it picked up after the explosion. I didn't think I could exactly *salvage* the film, but I knew I could definitely perk it up a little. It needed a title song. I'd done a nifty number called 'Star Wars (What Are They Good for)' for *The Phantom Menace*, but George Lucas (who didn't know a flumpet from a flugelhorn) rejected it. So I altered the melody enough to avoid Lucasfilm litigators, wrote some new lyrics, and sent it to Paul . . .

(Music should have a galloping feel, with occasional stabs of tuba)

Verse 1
Been down this well
With my big ol' axe,
It's a living hell,
Near broke my back.

Been searchin' for silver,
Now I'm drillin' for oil,
I'm a schemin' S.O.B.
And I won't be foiled.

Did a sketch of a well,
Then I got me a son,
Took the train into town
And I bought me a bun (from the buffet car).

Watch out, you suckers,
I ain't panning for dimes,
Gots crazy skills,
Gonna build me a mine.

Chorus
I ain't your friend,
No, I ain't your bud,
I'm Drillin' Dan Plainview
And There Will Be Blood.
Yes, There Will Be Blood.
Likes if you put a hammer through a haddock,
There Will Be Blood.

Verse 2
I've crawled on my belly
Like a goddamn snake,
Now I'm dinin' on jelly
And delicious-style steak.

Don't like no boy preachers
Rappin' God's commands,
'Im preachin' to my workers,

Im-pedin' my plans.

Got a derrick this high,
Done you seen my tower?
Then it blew its top,
Like a hot shit shower.

Religion's like water
And I'm like oil,
The two don't mix
'Cos I'm hydrophobic.

Bridge
I'm liquid (at ambient temperatures),
I'm black as night (presuming no light pollution),
I'm soluble (in organic solvents),
And I'm ready for a fight (with that fraudulent boy
    priest).

Chorus
I'll drink his milkshake
Like it's a choco-malt flood,
I'm droolin', but I ain't foolin'
Cos There Will Be Blood.
Yes, There Will Be Blood.
Likes if you puts your pecker in a thresher,
There Will Be Blood.

I'll drink his milkshake,
Won't show him no love,
I'll bisect his nut
And There Will Be Blood.
Oh, There Will Be Blood.

Likes if you drags your unprotected anus 'cross
     some jagged flint,
There Will Be blood.

Though I'm in a mighty big house,
I feels me diminished,
This alley's red runnin'
And I guess I'm finished!
'Cos There Will Be Blood.
Yes, There Will Be Blood.
Likes if your arm is inexpertly amputated,
There Will Be Blood.

And he went for Jonny Greenwood.

XI. PAUSE FOR THOUGHT

– Why would Ayoade concentrate so much energy on an article alluding to the (presumably by time of printing) disbanded group The Script?

– What did Danny O'Donoghue ever do to Ayoade?

– How well does Ayoade disguise his 'voice' when writing from the perspective of other 'characters'?

– Do you think that Ayoade secretly wants to write something that people actually *like* and this is why he's so hostile to the idea of a popular comedy?

– How believable are Ayoade's conceits? Are they believable at all?

– What do you think these articles reveal about Ayoade's anxieties concerning writing? Is he right to be worried? Exactly how worried should he be?*

* You may need extra paper for this one.

XII. SPACE FOR NOTES

The G(REA)t Pretender:
Ayoade on Acting*

<hr />

* R. E. A. being Ayoade's initials. His full name? Richard Einstein Ayoade.

I. AN AUDITION

Last month I put myself on tape* for a post-apocalyptic action comedy called *Boom Goes the Neighborhood!*. Herewith some edited highlights from the director's notes:

- Duder! I'm a HUGE fan of yours – so sorry to make you go on tape – it's just a formality. Seriously. Everyone here in L.A. LOVES you!!! Can't wait to see it!!!!
- Hey! The tape was really great for a tape and I'm sure I can cut together moments from the tape to create something that works as a whole tape. The only thing is that you sort of do a weird thing where you show your teeth after you speak in a creepy way. Are they your teeth or are they a prop? If they're your teeth, do you have access to a dentist? If they were filed down a little and your gums were lowered, how long do you think it would take to heal? If you think less than a week maybe do it, but if not maybe try to keep your mouth closed when you speak.
- Actually I've looked at the tape again, and while your teeth are definitely disturbing, I think it may be more to do with the overall shape of your head. Is it because your hair is so

---

* This is less metaphysical than it sounds: it's an audition conducted remotely – a self-filmed screen test. These days it can be recorded on a video phone. Ayoade's casual use of the industry jargon 'put yourself on tape' speaks of a blinkered arrogance that steadily escalates throughout this Hollywood escapade.

high? Could you slick it back in some way but not so much that you look like the comic relief in a blaxploitation film? Perhaps you could do a few different versions, cutting half an inch off your hair each time? Thanks!

- It wasn't your hair. I can see why you keep it long. Your head doesn't make sense now as a head. But that's okay – we don't shoot for a couple weeks, so maybe start growing it back as of now. I'm sure we can use lights to hide your chin.
- Can you do it again but wear a different shirt? The one you wore sort of made you look like you were on fire. Thanks for sticking with this – I was able to watch most of that last tape sober.
- Is your voice naturally that nasal? Do you think you can speak so that it sounds less like the dialog is coming *out* of your nose?
- Your voice is now too deep. I don't have that good a treble control on my computer. I had to put my hand on the keyboard and guess what you were saying by the vibrations.
- No – wait – I didn't have the sound on. I think that was an earthquake.
- Is that the one way you have of acting? I looked on YouTube, and it seems that it is, but I just thought I'd ask. I love what you're doing, but I don't know that I'd feel comfortable filming it or showing it to others. Perhaps I can splice a performance together from individual syllables.
- So sorry you had to find out that way, man. Although you're similar, I just felt that Mr T had the edge.

II. TERMS OF ENGAGEMENT

In which Ayoade receives an update about the sci-com
Boom Goes the Neighborhood!.

DannytotheD
to me
Hey Kiddo,
You've got the gig! Mr T dropped out for artistic reasons and
'they've exhausted all other options'. Congratulations! Did
you get that box of luxury goods I sent? Because the post
here is terrible and you may not get it even though I definitely
sent it. So maybe the best thing is to imagine a really big box
of luxury goods and that's what I personally bought you as
a well-done-for-eventually-getting-the-part gift, but it's most
likely lost. So, sorry, I guess. And it's not the kind of thing
that'll turn up at the depot. Those people are scavengers and
will totally have taken everything so don't even try to trace it.
Anyway, I thought it best to write you about the contractual
deal I've made on *Boom!* because I figured that if I told
you on the phone, you'd get upset or I'd start giggling or
something. I've now perfected your signature, so you don't
even need to sign! It's already done! No need to contact me!

- It's a seven-month shoot in Kuwait. You're only needed
  for three days, but they're not sure which days they'll be.
  You'll be on a will-notify. That means every morning you
  make your way to the set and they'll let you know if they

have work for you that day. You'll also receive your bread ration and air-conditioning token.

– They are not willing to provide transportation, but it's only a four-mile hike straight up a main road, a tiny trek through a quarry/mine, and then a brief swim, depending on the tide. I said that'd be fine because you're getting a little chubby anyway, especially round the neck. You have a weak Norwegian chin, and the sooner you can start burning off that whale blubber, the better for you and the film.

– They will not pay for your family to come out with you. Are you close?

– I've got you accommodation in a very spirited area with great views of the neighboring transport options. And before you bring up the past again: yes, it does have a window this time. I think it also has a toilet near by. AND you're in walking distance from an IKEA (I know – there really is one in Kuwait)! You may hear occasional gunfire, but I'm told that as long as you stay away from the window and keep low you should be fine. By the way, I don't know if you do drugs, but apparently this is THE place to get them. (But make sure you don't get caught trafficking, because the death penalty still applies there, and, if killed, you will be in breach of contract.)

– They would rather not discuss the issue of remuneration at the moment. I agreed that as long as they could pay me the commission on what I ideally would have got you, I would be happy, and you would view this as an investment in your future.

– You will be billed in the title credits, but they are insisting on using your real name.

170

– Because you're using your own accent in the movie, they want you to use an accent of their choosing whenever you're off set. You will be followed to ensure compliance.

– You don't have to show your penis in the molestation scene, but they reserve the right to use a double, 'the ethnicity of which will be as close a match as can reasonably be sought from the local community'.

– There is now a molestation scene.

That's it! Have fun! No need to call! By the way, did you get my mail about their concerns regarding your 'womanly arms'?

III. ACTING THE PART

Things develop apace on apocalyptic bomb-com *Boom Goes the Neighborhood!*. I now have a new part: CHUBBY ALIEN. I'm relishing the role. Plus the scaly fat-suit and animatronic head I wear mean I'm able to do most scenes with my eyes closed, something that's usually very hard to justify. This morning I was even handed some lines! And although they will eventually be redubbed, I've been assured that my voice will be used as a 'guide'! Herewith said speech and some of my initial annotations.

CHUBBY ALIEN

My alien brethren and I have traveled through countless eons to make contact with you.[1] My people are a proud race,[2] which makes what I have to say doubly difficult. Zargfarst is dying and we need to harvest energy.[3] Inevitably,[4] this journey has used yet more energy. Your electric grid has proved too crude[5] for our advanced sensors, so we have been collecting batteries[6] to power the ship's particle refraculator. Now that the particle refraculation is almost complete,[7] we must let nothing stand in our way, not even the extinction of the plague that is the human race![8] Let the probing commence![9]

1 Therefore, he will be tired. Perhaps sit on a chair at this moment to emphasise his weariness. Is a long sigh too 'hack'? Note how well-spoken this alien is. He obviously did well in whatever education system they had on his planet. Or maybe these aliens have universally

higher standards of oratory? Perhaps your performance can straddle this crack of ambiguity . . .

2 Showing this pride is VITAL! Would it be too vulgar for the character to get an erection at this moment? In which of his penises? Must get on better terms with the man who works the levers.

3 Not to labour the point, but remember how EXHAUSTED *you* feel after a long trip, particularly on a coach. Just the smell of the seats. You can't read, all you can do is stare – it's prison.

4 And ironically!

5 It seems as though CHUBBY ALIEN is being a little pejorative here. Our grids are hardly crude, requiring as they do the stepping up and down of voltage via interconnected networks that deliver electricity from suppliers to consumers in a way that we've come to take for granted. I'd certainly like to see CHUBBY ALIEN offer up an alternative method of servicing our power needs!

6 RESEARCH, RESEARCH, RESEARCH! If you don't know a wet-cell battery from a molten-salt battery, the audience will laugh in your face. And, what's more, you'll deserve it!!

7 If the particles have refraculated, they must once have been unfraculated, or in a natural state of pre-refraculation. Visualise the particles fraculating and then refraculating before your astonished gaze. Ask the FX team to keep your middle eye STILL for this moment.

8 This is just plain rude! If it weren't for the so-called 'human plague' developing batteries in the C19th, they wouldn't have been able to power their ship's particle refraculator in the first place! Remember: you MUST defend your character! HE thinks he's right, even when he's being as short-sighted and ungracious as this.

9 What a shame to end a nuanced and layered speech with this kind of cheap shot.

IV. AN ACTOR ASKS

Stanislavski suggested that every actor should ask himself the following seven questions. As the artistic rigours mount on my current thespian engagement, the mid-apocalyptic rom-com *Boom Goes the Neighborhood!*, I turn to him for answers.

1. Who am I?

Who is this character? Who am I? Who are you? Isn't that the title of a Who record? Does this character even like The Who? Who *does* like The Who any more? Who do The Who think they are? Can two people still be The Who? Should they now call themselves The Two? Is it morbid to wonder who's next? Isn't *Who's Next* another one of their album titles? Do you think they called themselves The Who just for the punning opportunities? Is this line of questioning relevant to every character I play?

2. Where am I?

Why do I have to share a trailer with the toilet attendant? Why does the toilet attendant have a trailer? Wait: is my trailer a toilet? Could that explain the urinals and the constant influx of people coming in to do bottom time? Was the producer lying when he said that 'Everyone else's trailer is tiled as well'? But it makes me think: what is the bladder capacity of my character? Does it exceed my bladder capacity? If so, how can I play him and maintain the respect of those around me?

3. When?
When will I start work on this film? Is it normal to be called to rehearse every day and for the director to decide (every day) that maybe my lines can be 'just as easily conveyed by putting subtitles under the shot of the cat'? Isn't that what they do in trailers for indie romantic comedies? Isn't this meant to be a war film? Why have I never seen this 'cat'?

4. What do I want?
Is it *just* 'more lines'? Should I not worry about that and concentrate on saying the three lines I *do* have? Is it bad to nap between my lines? Should I only do that off camera? Is it worrying that I started off with ninety lines? Is the director being genuine when he says he wants to 'harness the power of my silence'? Is it a coincidence that each of my lines is a question? 'Hello?' 'Who's there?' And 'Do you think this will heal?'

5. Why do I want this?
And, moreover, why do I even bother getting up in the morning?

6. How will I achieve my goal?
Would it help to see this film in the bigger context of life? Does it really matter in the grand scheme of all eternity? Is there a grand scheme of all eternity? Who cares now I only have one line? 'Who's there?' – the *ultimate* philosophical question. Or just a good album title? Does the fact that my character detests atheists mean that he is in

175

fact an atheist? *I* think all this subtext is to be found in that one line I have, but are modern audiences too desensitised to appreciate all my layers?

7. What must I overcome?
And why is there so much of it?

V. PAUSE FOR THOUGHT

- How do these articles challenge traditional or stereo-typical views of Hollywood?

- Is it possible to take the idea of Ayoade as an actor at all seriously?

- Is there another name for what Ayoade does? If so, what?

- Could you describe Ayoade as a character actor? If so, what would you say his character was?

- In what way does Ayoade challenge the orthodoxy that actors should be able to play a variety of roles?

- Are there any clues in these articles as to how Ayoade still manages to get work?

VII. ACTING UP

My co-stars on *Boom Goes the Neighborhood!* have been beyond supportive of my fledgling flight into the apo-com-lyptic action genre, and many now know my name. And, from the start, one in particular has been marvellously vigilant in keeping the lines of communication with me open and clear (via his legal representatives). At their request, I am only permitted to reprint my own letters to them and not any correspondence written by them on behalf of their client (whose name is withheld, also at their request).

Many thanks for your recent letter.

No need to worry, I have already received the instruction not to address your client verbally except via his assistant. The 'good morning' I uttered was an error born of habit and not an attempt 'to ransack the foundations of [my] employment'. While avoiding *any* eye contact with your client during the scenes themselves may prove hard, I'm certainly looking forward to the challenge! Also, thanks in abundance for the further clarifications you graciously make in the enclosed appendix. I will not cross those particular boundaries again. In my dealings with other people a handshake has been viewed as a cordial gesture and not the 'epidermal defilement' referred to in your draft injunction. In future I will offer the quarter-bow that you so kindly suggest.

Might I make one small request in turn? Is there any way

179

that your client could stop practising golf during my takes? The metronome-like swish of metal behind the camera is distracting enough, but the constant cries of 'Fore!' make it near impossible to deliver dialogue.

Sincere supplications . . .

* * *

A thousand thank-yous for your recent communication.

I am well aware that your client is on a strict alfalfa and chlorophyll cleanse and that the smell of 'any food on [my] breath' must be 'fatally distracting' for him. However, your team's insistence that I 'stop eating for the duration of the production' is proving difficult. Yesterday I caved and ordered a double helping at the IKEA snack station. Forty meatballs. That's going to haunt me, and those around me, for several days to come. However, I can assure you that I will restrict any liquid intake on set to the bare minimum and if driven by sheer madness to 'consume solids' I will indeed do so in the 'privacy of the crew toilet'. Can I take this opportunity to mention that dribbling a basketball off camera may, if anything, be even more disruptive than the putting practice?

An armoire of apologies . . .

* * *

A rolodex of *remerciement* for your timely epistle.

I suppose, given the physical distance you'd like me to maintain from your client, it's tricky to know exactly *when* he's breathing in, and so for me 'not to exhale at any time that [your] client is inhaling' requires a synchronisation that may be beyond my physical capacities. Perhaps this particular rhythm was what he was trying to imply with the

180

golf swings? And while the suggestion that 'perhaps [I] don't breathe at all' seems simple, it's one that I feel may be tricky in conjunction with your client's parallel suggestion, communicated via his security chief, for me to 'go fuck [myself] in the mouth'. Perhaps I must indeed endeavour to view such outbursts as 'the gift of fear'.

    In faithful expectation of ever closer ties . . .

VIII. CHARACTER ACTING

The word is out about my nuanced and game-changing performance in the sci-fi romp-com *Boom Goes the Neighborhood!*. I've been deluged with suggestions for what I might do next, some more aggressive than others. But before I even consider a new role I always make extensive notes and character analyses. Only then can I start my many metamorphoses.

CHARACTER: CASHIER
Note the absence of the definite article. It's not THE CASHIER. It's not A CASHIER. It's CASHIER. Pinter would have been proud: after all, he was a great writer. CASHIER is mythic. CASHIER is unknowable. He (or she – I don't know what gender I'll play CASHIER as) stands for all cashiers. Question: if Ewan McGregor were playing CASHIER, what accent would he use? Would it be the accent he employed in *The Ghost Writer*? What accent was that? Further thought: perhaps Apple could develop an iPhone app to help you identify what accent Ewan McGregor is doing (when acting).

CHARACTER: UNCLE 1
Clearly he's not the only uncle in our little drama, but he is the first. Hunt for clues in the script. One stage direction says, '*He's kind of old-looking*'. How does he feel about ageing and mortality? In the scene where he says, 'Helluva

cake!' does he mean it? Is it really the 'best damn wedding cake I ever tasted'? There are no other lines as such, but is it too much to detect a moment of menace when he '*scratches his balls, oblivious*'? Or a trace of poignancy when he '*trips over the HEAVY ORNAMENT and falls on his ass to the amusement of everyone*'?

CHARACTER: QUIET DUDE

Already there's conflict: quiet v. dude. A battle rages in QUIET DUDE. A duel between two irreconcilable and oppositional forces. This part will be a continuation of the psychological exploration I began when I played BORING-SEEMING ZOO KEEPER in *Zoo Cops*.

(Note: I'm assuming QUIET DUDE is a 'he'. Dude-ishness suggests cocksure masculinity, but one should always discuss this with the director to avoid embarrassment on set. Many's the time I've arrived at a shoot only to be rebuked for not being a woman.)

CHARACTER: WEIRD MAN

Judgement has no place in my process. For me he's MAN. With all his complications, beauty and savagery. Question: if Tom Cruise were playing this part, at what point would he take his top off? Further question: if I were Tom Cruise, would I even bother wearing tops, or would I just stay home and play with my tits?

CHARACTER: THIN PILOT

The stress of his many missions has left him wan and emaciated. He's ever ready to lay down his life for others, selfless, saint-like. He has a poet's hands, and if he ever points one of his delicate fingers, it is to question authority or wipe away beads of sweat from a dying rear-gunner, never

183

IX. A PLUM PART

In which Ayoade receives an email from his US agent.

DannytotheD
to me
Hey Ronald!
Long time! Hope you're not dead or something! Just to
say an exciting casting opportunity's come in from James
Cameron, the guy who made *Avatar* (I know – it's amazing
to me that a man came up with that – I thought it was made
by computers or something!). They'd like you to self-tape
because they're going to decide this in the next four minutes.
So do your prep and then record yourself on one of the
recording devices you probably have set up on a tripod next
to where you are.

   Jim says he's looking for SENSITIVITY, PROWESS,
and DANGER, but also BALLS. You're PERSON WHO
INTERRUPTS TARQKONIUM EXPERT. And please
remember to press 'record'. I missed the birth of my son that
way and now all I've got is the child but no footage of its birth
and I don't know who I'm angriest with – the kid, my wife, the
elite team of nurses, my phone, or my piece-of-shit thumb.
Here's the scene. Good luck, pig!

TARQKONIUM EXPERT

All we have are half-thoughts and pipe dreams.

FEDERAL LIAISON OFFICER

I don't like dreams, I've always hated pipes, and if
I have a thought I want it to be like my wife: full-
fat. So stop telling me fairy tales and start telling me
facts, you fairy.

TARQKONIUM EXPERT

I ain't no fairy and I hate pipes as much as you do. I
lost my cousin to a pipe.

FEDERAL LIAISON OFFICER

In case you hadn't noticed, there's an eon-old inter-
galactic war on, so please excuse my blunt talk and
casual homophobia.

TARQKONIUM EXPERT

(*Turns and looks at the decayed remnants of 'B'
Quadrant, charred red by centuries of laser blasts*)
I never should've written that pamphlet on ultra-
explosive energy fission! I meant it for purely scien-
tific, non-war purposes.

FEDERAL LIAISON OFFICER

That little leaflet is the only thing keeping you
from doing hard 'T' on Neptron Nine. So spit it,
sister.

TARQKONIUM EXPERT

I ain't your sister, mister.

FEDERAL LIAISON OFFICER
I know. I was an only child. Still am.

*A moment. They understand. This war is ruining
everything.*

TARQKONIUM EXPERT
(*resolved*)
Tarqkonium is a highly unstable compound.
Its sub-electron structure can be disengaged by
sarcasm.

FEDERAL LIAISON OFFICER
Sarcasm?

TARQKONIUM EXPERT
It's a highly sensitive compound.

FEDERAL LIAISON OFFICER
Yeah. I know. I was being sarcastic.

TARQKONIUM EXPERT
Oh. That didn't really come across. It sounded like a
question.

FEDERAL LIAISON OFFICER
Look, buddy, I'm just doing my job of federally liais-
ing. Do you think I really give a squirt about some
crummy compound that didn't get enough titty milk
from Mommy?

TARQKONIUM EXPERT
Sorry, are you still being sarcastic? I'm not sure

187

whether you're quipping, being rhetorical, or refusing to back down over the sarcasm thing.

A slight, weedy man enters the lab.

PERSON WHO INTERRUPTS
TARQKONIUM EXPERT
Am I interrupting?

Cameron can write, huh?! BTW, this script's top secret. After
you've read this you should probably bury your computer in a
wood and then go buy another one.

X. ACTING, WITH SEAN PENN

Sean Penn and I have been in regular contact for years. I've worked with him both as an acting coach and, more recently, a kayaking companion. One of my first recommendations (after urging him to work on his capsize recovery) was that he keep a diary. Initially, he just took mine and refused to return it but, after an emotionally charged exchange about word usage, he agreed to write a journal of his own (I was allowed my own diary back every other weekend). I now share (for money) some extracts from his time working on the film *This Must Be the Place*, in which he plays a former rock star who looks and dresses exactly like Robert Smith from The Cure.*

Monday

After literally *hours* I think I've got my make-up just right. Now I can concentrate on acting for godssakes already. Maybe I'll do a voice. I don't know yet. I'm tired and I need to wipe my face.

Tuesday

It's actually really hard for goths in summer. These jumpers are murder in the heat. I have a whole new level of respect for The Sisters of Mercy. Perhaps I should bring out a summer goth line. Still black, but looser fitting smocks/cargo pants.

* This is no joke – Google-image it.

Stuff you can wear to the beach, but still look suicidal. I could call it the Sean Penn Summer Goth Collection. And if people don't like it they can suck my dick.

Wednesday
Just woke up from a dream. Or did I? Perhaps I'm asleep now. I guess what I'm saying is that we all need to wake up, before more people die from apathy. (Can people die from apathy? I don't know – must get my assistant to google 'apathy + dying from it'. I'd text him, but I just gave my Blackberry to a homeless person – which reminds me, I need to wash my hands.)

Thursday (middle of the night)
Still pissed about the *Tree of So-Called Life*. What happened to my sweet subplot about being an awesome architect? All I do is stare out of an elevator window like I've got an anal infection.

Friday
What a day! I acted so much before lunch that I ended up needing to eat two puddings after my chicken kievs: a custard-y one that had sultanas in and then a lighter one that may have been meringue (though I couldn't be sure because I still had the taste of the first one in my mouth). They were both good, but I felt heavy in the afternoon. I used that feeling, though, and by mid-afternoon I did a really kick-butt piece of acting where I looked all calm and then shouted really loud and then sat down and cried in a corner and didn't even care if I dribbled. And although the scene was just meant to be me having a quiet bath, I think I made a brave choice that was maybe even more valid and true and brave than anyone's ready to accept at this stage in the

190

evolution of our process. Who knows if they'll use it in the end? I don't even know if they were pointing the camera at me, that's how into it I was. Who gives a fuck? I'm Sean Penn.

XI. PAUSE FOR THOUGHT

Okay. No questions here. Just take a breath. This is about *recovery.*

You made it.

I *told* you it'd be tough.

Only one more part to go.

Wherein we take what we've learned . . .

. . . and we make our final approach.

Use your 'Space for Notes' to jot down any feelings you may have as to the validity of this diversion, then march on.

XII. SPACE FOR NOTES

PART 2C*

STORMING THE PENTAGON

or

DISCONTINUING THE DEKALOG

* Or not 2C?

Re(cap)itulation

It is with mixed feelings that I arrange to meet Ayoade for, potentially, the last time. What would these conversations add up to? Had he got close to me in order to keep me at arm's length? Would I keep the baby?*

I want to end my journey by reflecting on a creative mystery. I'd set out to discover a legend but I'd found a man – a man whose body of work (and body) fearlessly seeks to unravel the mysteries of the human condition. I'd unearthed an emotion-laden man, weighted down by fury (and his body). I'd explored a man who had failed to illicit any interest from other people in that body of work (or (heavy) body). I'd encountered a man capable of great acts of kindness – the fact that he chooses never to perform any great acts of kindness only adds to his mystery.

I'd discovered a director.

I'd wrestled with a writer.

I'd acknowledged an 'actor'.

I'd come upon them in person, in streets and bars, in their fiction and in my dreams, in byways and (in a near collision) on highways. Yes, I had met many men.

I'd met only one Ayoade.

I spend my days agonising over titles, none of which seem to adequately register the aspirations and achievements of our tête-à-têtes:

---

* I wrote this sentence before I realised I wasn't pregnant (see earlier note). I decided to keep it in because I have a word count to make.

INSIDE AYOADE: A MEETING OF MEN

TALKING WITH AYOADE: EXAMINING THE CRAFT

IN CONVERSATION WITH AYOADE: EXPLORING
THE JOURNEY

WALKING WITH AYOADE: THE FIRST STEP STARTS INSIDE

AYOADE UNDER THE MICROSCOPE: SPEAKING
TO THE SPECIMEN

AYOADE ON FILM: PRISING THE PRISM

THE AYOADE FILM READER: THE GENESIS OF GENIUS

THE BURDEN OF BRAVERY: AN ATLAS OF AYOADE

LOVING YOUR ALBATROSS: AYOADE, ANXIETY,
AND THE NEW AGE OF NARRATIVE

Perfectionism – that uniquely Ayoadean albatross –
had flopped onto my own private deck. But there was no
time to engage with that particular Ancient Rhyme. I had
an appointment to keep.
And off went I.

INTERVIEW TEN

The journey so far; staying excited; keeping grounded;
facing challenges; a title; a revelation

'. . . I'll die before I self-impede . . .'

INT. BATHROOM – I GUESS IT'S NIGHT, BUT WHO'S
COUNTIN'?

*Old romantics that we are, Ayoade and I decide to meet
in the place where our badinage began: my toilet. By this
time we are so relaxed we are both able to shower openly
(both emotionally and actually) in front of one another. I
ask simple questions, without theme, relying on Ayoade
as the final linking thread.*

NO CAMERAS. NO LIGHTS. ALL ACTION.

AYOADE   **How far do you feel you've travelled in your
               filmmaking career?**

AYOADE   I've made two films now, so I feel I've
               earned the right to pause and reflect on
               my achievements. Put it this way – I've got
               enough air miles now to get to Birmingham
               and back in business class.

AYOADE   **How do you think history will judge your
               films?**

AYOADE   I think *history* will be given perspective
               by my films. In fact – and I urge you to
               capitalise this in your transcription –

I THINK MY FILMS ARE THE FILMS
BY WHICH *HISTORY* WILL BE
JUDGED.

AYOADE   **What were the first films you saw?**

AYOADE   *Platoon. Driller Killer. Muppets Take
Manhattan.*

AYOADE   **Do you ever get bored?**

AYOADE   I'm on the verge now.

AYOADE   **Do you consider yourself a genius? You've
been called a brooding genius by *Film
Flap* . . .**

AYOADE   I don't know that I brood. I just
occasionally take time out to silently
consider the specific ways in which others
have wronged me.

AYOADE   **What words do you think best describe you?**

AYOADE   'Vital', 'urgent', 'beacon', 'potent',
'eternal'.

AYOADE   **How do you stay grounded?**

AYOADE   My own humanity keeps me grounded.
Friends keep me grounded. Sometimes I'll
be at a friend's house and the doorbell will
ring and I'll be like, 'Don't worry – *I'll*

get the door.' Even though that doesn't make any sense! My time is much more valuable than the time of anyone else in the house, and I'm so famous that whoever is at the door is probably going to go into a meltdown and be all 'OH MY GOD! I LOVE YOU!!' but I think by pretending – if only for a brief and ultimately pointless moment – that I'm not more important than everyone else, I think I experience this tremendous feeling of *groundedness*. Of what it must feel like to be boring and ordinary and not even have an assistant to open the door for you and say, 'I'm sorry but Mr Ayoade is busy right now, can I take a message?'

Or sometimes I'll visit my mother and *I'll* take out the rubbish! It's amazing – she's in her seventies, retired, she gets *all day* to rest, and I'm doing this utterly everyday-type chore. It's actually hilarious. I remember being there this one time – it was drizzling – and I was trying to open the lid of this big wheelie bin, but there was a gate in front of it, so it was kind of awkward because I had a rubbish bag, and one of those recycling bags as well, and the recycling bag split and I thought, 'Fuck this! I should be inside sitting down thinking of scripts – what the hell is my piece-of-shit mum even doing?!'

AYOADE   **Right . . .**

AYOADE   That's the end of the story.

AYOADE   Oh, sorry. I got the rhythm wrong. I thought you were going to say, 'But then I realised I was overreacting,' or something –

AYOADE   Overreacting? Are you fucking kidding me? There was gross, rotten food all over the floor. There was gross, rotten food on *me* and I don't think I need to repeat the fact that it was *drizzling*. I'm all for being grounded, but I'm not a slave. I'm not Chiwetel Ejiofor. I'm a free man! I should never have been out there in the first place. It was the craziest thing that's ever happened to me.

AYOADE   Who challenges you?

AYOADE   I find that the person who challenges me best is me. I know which buttons to press, but also when to insist I take a beach break. But you know what? I'm going to say something very gracious now: you challenge me.

There is a moment.

AYOADE   Thank you.

And another.

AYOADE   I mean it. What's inspired me so much about doing this book is that you are another facet of me. Obviously, by being in the 'journalist' role, you are the most weak, facile and spineless side of me, but you're still me. You have a *type* of insight. Clearly no one can completely know me, not even me, so you get it wrong, you're afraid to fully engage. You're shy of a full celebration of my gifts, but at least you dare approach. A lot of people who *aren't me* daren't even approach!

AYOADE   **Well, I'm pleased I did.**

AYOADE   I was thinking about a title: *Ayoade on Ayoade*.

AYOADE   **I like it.**

AYOADE   But it does have a flaw.

AYOADE   **It seems perfect, though.**

AYOADE   It does seem perfect. But it isn't. Its weakness is that it suggests simple duality, as though there are only two sides to me. And that is insufficient. There are at least seventeen sides to me. If anything, this book should be called *Ayoade to the Power of Seventeen*. But I don't want to alienate people who don't have the mathematical knowledge that I do.

AYOADE   ***Ayoade on Ayoade* is simple. Elegant. I don't think it impedes your multifaceted-ness.**

205

AYOADE   Good. Because I'll die before I self-impede.
           Are we done?

He does not wait for an answer.

*He strides over and locks me in a power-hug of such
ferocity that I later thought it prudent to get a chest X-ray.
I cannot tell if there are tears dripping from Ayoade's eyes,
or if it is the sting of Lemon Refresh shower foam, but I
start to cry as well. He releases me from the minute-long
embrace, shakes me vigorously by the temples, and claps
my ear so hard that it will ring for an entire weekend.
Our goodbye is wrenching, if inaudible; our encounter the
highlight of my life so far. Its legacy? Well, you're holding
it in your hands. It's this book. These words.*

Ayoade on Ayoade.*

*Ayoade begins to dress himself. First his pants; then his
jeggings; and, with a final flourish, his business wig.
Solemnly, he extends a digit and gently depresses the
'stop' button of my tape recorder.*

Click.

He turns and leaves.

Slam.

Snap to black.

* If only!

I am left alone, no longer wretched in my nakedness, but with my full self proud and revealed. I look at the mirror, heavy with steam, dancing with droplets. A face appears.

It is my face. A simple, ordinary face.

For I am not Ayoade.

Or maybe I'm just not the kind of Ayoade I thought I was. I am a man. I am a woman. I am a child. I am you, the reader. I am a human being in the twenty-first century whose thirst for Ayoade is unquenchable. And is it not that yearning – that *lack* in all of us – that sense that *something's missing* – that brought us to Ayoade in the first place? Are we not all Ayoade? Is Ayoade not all of us?

Had I dreamt my entire encounter with Ayoade, or dreamt it only in part? Or was it all a dream *within* a dream, like *Inception* by Christopher Nolan, our generation's Kubrick? All I know is that there *was* an encounter. And it's changed me. It's changed me in a way that's deep and true.

Perhaps the man I met was Ayoade. Perhaps he was not. But then, my friends, what would be the difference? For we are all held together by cinema – that flickering kiss – that infinite screen – that wall stretching to the beyond that separates us just as it binds us together in an everlasting embrace.

No fade. Only light.

A
P
(PEN)
DI
(X)*

* If you've been reading this book correctly, you should be done by now. Congrats. Have a candle-lined bubble bath. Skip to p. 301 for a final adieu. If this is the first time you've been to this section, you've failed me (see note on p. ii). Please re-read the book again properly.

Ayoade on Awards

People often say that the lower the art form, the more awards ceremonies there are for that art form.

But the people who say this have never won an award.

They are losers, by literal definition, sadly incapable of grasping that awards are one of the few ways we have left of deciding what and who is of value. The only thing more satisfying than winning an award is a favourable mention in a broadsheet newspaper.

In fact, if Van Gogh had ever received an award or been singled out for positive comment by a journalist, perhaps he wouldn't have gone out into a field and shot himself in the chest. Do you think Cameron Diaz would go out into a field and shoot *her*self in the chest? Of course not. Because, if she ever felt even the tiniest bit sad, she'd remember that in 1996 she received an award at the ShoWest Convention for 'Female Star of Tomorrow', an honour that paid off a decade later when she was nominated for a People's Choice Award for 'Favorite Leading Lady'. *The People's Choice.* That means that of all the leading ladies in the *entire world* that had been in high-profile films with a significant PR and marketing spend in 2006, she was chosen, by *all people*, as one of the three best. She wouldn't even get as far as her gun cabinet before being buffeted back by soothing gales of pride. Not even the fact that Reese Witherspoon actually *beat* her to the award would make her want to jam a pistol into her ribcage and discharge its deadly cargo.

So in readiness for the time when YOUR life is validated by a prize at a televised awards ceremony, here is a helpful template for accepting it with recordable dignity.

– This was a complete surprise! I can't believe I'm even here in front of [NAME OF PERSON]

– You [REACTION SHOT OF PERSON] have been such an inspiration to me! And I mean, just to be nominated alongside [NAMES OF TWO, THREE OR FOUR PEOPLE WHO HAVE NOT WON] is mind-blowing.

– I know I only have [AMOUNT OF TIME] so I'll try my best to be brief. I hope I don't cry. [BRIEFLY LOOK LIKE YOU MIGHT CRY. ALLOW TIME FOR SYMPATHETIC AUDIENCE MURMUR.]

– It's so humbling to receive this [NAME OF AWARD], especially when it's voted for by [NAME OF ORGANISATION]. The [NAME OF ORGANISATION] has always been a beacon of [NOUN] and . . . [APPLAUSE.]

– I'm truly, truly honoured. [HUMBLE HAND GESTURE.]

– But of course I could not have done this alone [PAUSE TO CREATE A FACE THAT LOOKS CONSISTENT WITH THIS STATEMENT]. I would not be here at all if it were not for [VARIOUS PEOPLE] and most importantly [SEXUAL PARTNER/DEITY/HARVEY WEINSTEIN].

– It's awards like [NAME OF AWARD] that allow us all to

212

keep doing what we do [DO NOT MENTION WHAT YOU DO IN CASE IT SEEMS TRIVIAL IN SUCH CLOSE PROXIMITY TO THE AWARD], so I must give genuine thanks to [NAME OF ORGANISATION] for giving me this wonderful [JOVIAL DESCRIPTION OF AWARD], which I will display proudly on/in my [HUMOROUSLY INCONGRUOUS LOCATION] . . . Er . . . [LAUGHTER] . . .

– Thanks so, *so* much . . .

[HUMBLE HALF-BOW, SKIP OFF WITH FURTHER QUARTER-BOW.]

Ayoade: Quizmaster

This is a transcript of the questions Ayoade set for the Tri-Annual Quiz-A-Thon held by the British Independent First Feature in A Realist Tradition awards (The BIFFARTs).

Tragically, halfway through James Nesbitt's opening monologue, a highly localised fire sparked. It melted the vodka luge* and ruined several sea-bass parcels. In an attempt to avert disaster, one prominent jury member stripped to the waist and frenziedly wafted the flames with her jacket. Unfortunately, Tilda's tunic was made of a highly flammable midnight-blue crêpe and went up like a hairball. The jacket contained the answers to the quiz. Luckily, Nesbitt was still in possession of the questions, and was willing to license them back to us for a moderate fee. Here they be:

What is Steven Spielberg's preferred method of birth control?

Who is director Steve McQueen's famous namesake?

---

* Vodka luges have been a fixture on the UK 'party scene' since the early nineties, a boom time for culture and artistry. A 'luge', also known as an 'ice luge' or 'vodka luge', is an ice sculpture containing a narrow channel through which liquid (ordinarily a spirit such as vodka) is dispensed into the waiting mouth of the 'luge-ist'. There is no need for the vodka luge to exist, except as a clear and urgent signal that you are in the wrong place.

Why won't Quentin Tarantino eat guacamole after dusk?

In what way is Mike Leigh different from a cult leader?

True or false: Ridley Scott's middle name is Didley?

Which leading figure in the film industry likes hearing jokes at their expense?

Can you name one successful and respected screenwriter?

Whatever happened to the actor Tom Hanks?

From what source does Robert Rodriguez get his confidence?

What actor, aside from Sean Connery, could get away with doing the same accent his whole career?

Why do people think it's possible to make a good Godzilla film?

Has any film ever been made that's better than the worst episode of *Columbo*?

What would possess someone to rewatch *Ordinary People*?

Who would win in a fight between Joe Pesci and Joe Pasquale?

Ayoade acted as Question Master for the Halloween quiz-off at the FilmFlam BamBam Website Contributors' Breakfast Breakdown, conducted by group Skype, on 31 October 2013. Ayoade was offline for the actual quiz, but personally posted the following message via his nephew.

'Gad tidings, Skype Pals. What better way to celebrate Halloween than with this chilling collection o' terrifying trivia questions? Write your answers on the undead souls o' the vanquished (or double-spaced on lined paper) and post to Richard Ayoade, c/o the Metaphysics and Eschatology Dept, the Richard Ayoade Foundation, Wrexham Division, Wrexham Industrial Estate, Wrexham. Please keep your answers as brief as possible (e.g. Q: Why were the actors in the film *Cloverfield* not given a script before they agreed to do the project? A: In case they read it.)

– What are the better ways to celebrate Halloween than this chilling collection o' terrifyingly unimportant trivia questions?

– As long as it's night, are vampires able to use tanning beds?

– Which Finnish frightener was set in a salmon farm? Was it (A) *The Deadly Salmon*; (B) *They Called Him Salmon*; (C) *I Was a Teenage Salmon Farmer*; (D) *Hell-sinki*?

– What is the killer's ethnically appropriate choice of weapon in the slasher flick *St Patrick's Day*?

– At what point during the filming of *Bride of Chucky* did those involved decide to keep on filming?

– What is the precise wattage of 'the shining' in the film *The Shining*?

– Can ANYONE remember ANYTHING that happened in ANY ONE of the *Nightmare on Elm Street* films?

– Why is Freddy Krueger's skin so susceptible to angry flare-ups? Is it possible he's allergic to wool?

– Can you think of a good reason to remake *The Texas Chainsaw Massacre*?

– Why did the makers of *Friday the 13th* choose to start their franchise with its twelfth sequel?

– Since when did zombies get so fast?

– In the film *The Exorcist* why are the priests so frightened of exercise?

– During which time of the year is the film *Halloween* set?

– Can you understand why they made a fifth *Scary Movie*?

– Can you understand why they made a first *Scary Movie*?

– Is it possible to be a Mistress of Suspense?

– What was the name of Rosemary's Baby's mother?

– In the film *Rosemary's Baby*, given that he's the father, why doesn't Satan attend the birth? Or at least send a note?

– In the film *The Mummy*, who is The Daddy?

– What emotion is a central theme in the film *The Terror*?

– Which Portuguese eco-horror features a soundtrack by Right Said Fred?

– Lon Chaney, the Man of a Thousand Faces, actually only had one face. But which one was it?

– Is it true that the shower scene in *Psycho* was originally meant to take place in a tapas bar and that instead of being repeatedly knifed to death, Janet Leigh's character simply enjoyed a wide variety of appetizers in pleasant surroundings?

– For what reason did they release the behind-the-scenes documentary of *The Blair Witch Project* instead of the actual film?

– Why have there been so few horror films about snails?

For one glorious summer Ayoade landed the much-envied job of writing the 'Did You Know?!?' questions that were projected onto the cinema screen while the curtains half closed in order to fully reopen for the adverts immediately prior to the pre-snack-break trailers before the main feature at the Bury St Edmunds CineStation. The post also entitled him to a Premium Platinum Maxi-Pass and 25 per cent off jumbo drinks. Here is a selection of Ayoade's favourite facts from that season.

Did you know . . . Stanley Kubrick played the bass-guitar riff in *Seinfeld* . . .?!?

Did you know . . . George Lucas was the original shark in *Jaws*, but had to be replaced when it was discovered he rusted in seawater . . .?!?

Did you know . . . the working title of *The Godfather* was *Godfather* . . .?!?*

Did you know . . . Charlie Chaplin was allergic to bread rolls . . .?!?**

Did you know . . . Walt Disney's film *Fantasia* is mainly a cartoon about a mouse . . .?!?

Did you know . . . no one really likes *The Rocky Horror Picture Show* . . .?!?

Did you know . . . Sean Connery turned down Dustin Hoffman's part in *Straw Dogs* because the lead character wasn't sufficiently sexist . . .?!?

Did you know . . . James Cameron's *Avatar* is the only film whose entire plotline is listed in the 'goofs' section of IMDB . . .?!?

* The inclusion of the definite article was suggested by Brian De Palma.
** Between each take of the famous 'dance of the bread rolls' he had to be covered entirely in natural yoghurt until the swelling subsided.

Did you know . . . *The Great Escape* was originally about landscape gardening . . .?!?*

Did you know . . . the original Tin Man in *The Wizard of Oz* suffered from painful and sudden erections . . .?!?**

Did you know . . . Ridley Scott has never been wrong, except for one time when he briefly doubted whether he was right . . .?!?

Did you know . . . Gene Kelly was frightened of his own feet . . .?!?

Did you know . . . Sigourney Weaver is Steven Seagal's uncle . . .?!?

Did you know . . . Woody Allen's real name is Chuck the Truck . . .?!?***

Did you know . . . an anagram of Fargo is Argof . . .?!?

Did you know . . . when Steven Spielberg showed John Williams a cut of *Schindler's List*, Williams was so moved he couldn't finish his chicken-dipper bucket . . .?!?

Did you know . . . *Cowboys & Aliens* received a theatrical release . . .?!?

---

* The POW camp was added in during editing.
** Although they lasted no more than four seconds, the clanging sound they caused within his costume became so disruptive that he was fired.
*** Allen changed his name in order to avoid any confusion between himself and motor vehicles designed to transport cargo.

Did you know . . . Jaden Smith is the son of the actor Will Smith . . .?!?

Did you know . . . in order to prepare for his role in *Random Hearts*, Harrison Ford glanced through the script . . .?!?

Did you know . . . *K-19: The Widowmaker* is an actual film . . .?!?

Did you know . . . Al Pacino privatised himself in 1986 and was bought out by Robert De Niro . . .?!?*

That autumn, Ayoade moved to the Bury St Edmunds Arts Cinétèque. As such, these questions display a bias to the perceived tastes of its clientele. Ayoade's tenure here was also brief, after he abused his Salted Almond Discount Badge.

Did you know . . . Pedro Almodóvar is gay?

Did you know . . . Michelangelo Antonioni didn't design all of the Sistine ceiling?

Did you know . . . Brigitte Bardot isn't always racist?

Did you know . . . Ingmar Bergman has had TWO different chunky sweaters named after him?**

* When the two actors appeared together in *Heat*, De Niro was prosecuted for insider trading.
** 'The Ingmar' and 'The Bergman'.

Did you know . . . Robert Bresson loved to play the bongos?

Did you know . . . Claude Chabrol was scared of hoovers?

Did you know . . . David Cronenberg directed the pilot episode of *Frasier*?

Did you know . . . Catherine Deneuve could've been a model?

Did you know . . . Rainer Werner Fassbinder had his own range of ring binders: Fassbinder's Ringbinders?

Did you know . . . William Friedkin is able to speak quietly?

Did you know . . . Michael Haneke has never been a guest on *Alan Carr: Chatty Man*?

Did you know . . . Werner Herzog is too self-conscious to eat Wiener Hotdogs?

Did you know . . . Spike Lee has his own money?

Did you know . . . David Lynch is obsessed with coffee?

Did you know . . . Jim Jarmusch doesn't like being in prison?

Did you know . . . Wong Kar-wai is the majority shareholder in Wonga.com?

Did you know . . . Krzysztof Kieślowski invented Space Invaders?

Did you know . . . Fritz Lang didn't need to wear a monocle; he just liked balancing things on his face?

Did you know . . . Mike Leigh is best friends with Michael Bay? They met through a mutual interest in their own first names.

Did you know . . . Sergio Leone was Welsh?

Did you know . . . Ken Loach has seen Usher in concert over fifty times?

Did you know . . . Yasujiro Ozu's *Tokyo Story* was originally entitled *Here Come the In-laws!*?

Did you know . . . Alexander Payne gets violently carsick?

Did you know . . . Roman Polanski sometimes has sex with adults?

Did you know . . . Satyajit Ray invented the wah-wah pedal?

Did you know . . . Satyajit Ray used his wah-wah pedal to leave funny answerphone messages?

Did you know . . . Jean Renoir's mantra was 'always give it 110 per cent'?

Did you know . . . Jacques Rivette films are often used in outpatient clinics as emergency muscle relaxants?

Did you know . . . Martin Scorsese doesn't even like pizza?

Did you know . . . Martin Scorsese still hasn't seen *Pain & Gain*?

Did you know . . . Martin Scorsese prefers watching films on his iPhone?

Did you know . . . Oliver Stone doesn't have an opinion on some matters?

Did you know . . . Andrei Tarkovsky briefly dated Gloria Estefan?

Did you know . . . François Truffaut's *Jules et Jim* was originally called *Two Guys and a Little Lady*?

Did you know . . . Agnès Varda isn't an anagram?

Did you know . . . Lars von Trier won't touch his own penis?

Did you know . . . Lars von Trier is a practising bishop?

Did you know . . . Lars von Trier's real name is Piers?

Extracts from Ayoade's Four-Volume Malick Parody, *The (Not So!) Secret Correspondence of Terrence Malick (As Told to Richard Ayoade)*

Terrence Malick, the reclusive director of such masterpieces as *Badlands*, *Days of Heaven* and *The Thin Red Line*, is about to release his new film, *The Tree of Life*. To the stupefaction of many, Malick was addicted to Twitter throughout the filming of his latest opus. Under the username MagicHourMan, he corresponded freely with those in his inner circle of 'tweeps', including Brad Pitt and Sean Penn. These excerpts show a relaxed Malick, one at odds with his highbrow public image . . .

Hey dudes – Tel here! Just finished new script. Can't wait to film this bitch and get it out to ya! Sorry it's taken so long. Writing's SOOOOOO hard!!!!!!!!

@misterbradpitt. Hey Brad, man! I love yr acting especially the acting you do with your face altho I also like the acting you do with the parts of your body that aren't your face . . . (contd)

@misterbradpitt . . . Like your arms/hands – say if you make a fist and punch someone or even point. Do you want to be in my new movie? It's about life! . . . (contd)

@**misterbradpitt** . . . And Sean Penn's going to be in it!!!!!!!
#dopeness

@**misterbradpitt** . . . Thanks! I like some of your work too!!

Waiting for funding. Need a haircut. Feel depressed.

Got funding!!!

Hey, who here's into Heidegger? Who's YOUR favorite
philosopher and why?!?!?!

Yeah, Plato's cool.

Tho Heidegger would always rag on the pre-Socratics.

In fact, your dog Heidegger didn't even like the term 'pre-
Socratics'.

@**misterbradpitt**. Really, isn't he mainly a bassist?

We start shooting tomorrow!! Wish me luck motherf**kers!!

Filming insects. BORING!!!! #fukdatsh*t

Who else likes crocodiles? They're freaky but cool too.
I wonder what they taste like? You'd think crunchy, but
probably it's like most meat.

Waiting for magic hour. Anyone know some good games for
the iPhone?

Thanks guyz! You're the bomb! Snake's some addictive shit!!!!!!

I wonder what happens when we die? #MysteriesOfLife

Today they let me hold the Steadicam – it's SO HEAVY. I feel bad for the MF who has to hold it. We've been filming for YEARS!!!!! #oops!

It's cool when the sky is orange or has pink bits in it. But I LOVE it when it's really RED!!!!

Man, who gave magic hour its name? It's so much shorter than an hour!!!! It's already dark and we got maybe two shots. Sh*t!!!!!!!!!!!!!!!!!!

I need a piss.

@**SeanPennTheActor**. Hey Sean, thanx for today! Great acting! I totally believed you were another person! Let's get tacos if you're not too tired!

@**misterbradpitt**. Don't cry about it. I just wasn't sure you'd be into tacos.

@**misterbradpitt**. You did fine.

@**misterbradpitt**. If there was a big problem I'd tell you.

Dinosaurs are sick.

Finished filming. Did kegs with @SeanPennTheActor @RealJessicaChastain. Think I'm gonna puke. #ShouldveDoneFewerKegs

In edit. Getting my snack on.

This is taking SO F**KING LONG to edit! There's so much film. Am SOOOO tired!!!!! #OnlyMyselfToBlame

Lens flare's cool.

I'm definitely going to use A LOT of voice-over. #GetOutOfJailFree

Need a haircut again. Think I'll get the barber to take more off this time. Sometimes I forget I have hair because I wear hats so much . . . (contd)

And then I look in the mirror just before I go to put my PJs on and I don't know who I am. #WhoAmI

Can't believe no one told me the White Stripes broke up! This is bullshit!! #Bummed

The *Tree of Life* is finished!!!!! Look out world: we're going to drop this sh*t like it's HOT!!!!!!!!! Can't wait to start the next one!!!!!!

Malick then quit Twitter for several months after a much-publicised spat with Brett Ratner. Until . . .

Guess who's back? Chicka chicka. #EminemShoutout

@Eminem. I know, dog! I'm dropping them like Woody!

@Eminem. I already have the Slaughterhouse LP!

@**Eminem**. I don't really do music videos.

@**Eminem**. Ha! Ha! Yeah!

If that shit's crazy, I don't want to be sane! RT: @**missalicesaysso**. Is it crazy to think that Terrence Malick would be amazing in bed?!

Finished editing. Coupla tricky phonecalls to make to @michaelsheen and @realrachelweisz. #IfYouDontWannaGetCutActBetter

He's okay. RT: @**jemimathemimer**. What's it like working with Ben Affleck?

I like butter. #RandomButTrue

Any ideas for a title?

That was a joke, I've got one.

To the Wonder!

Difficult to say what it means – you'll have to watch it!!!!!!!!

I like it. I'm going to bed . . .

Does anyone know what the best speakers to get for a laptop are?

Between $50–60 but if they're great maybe up to $80.

Thanks guys!

Just had a lovely pray. #GettingMyGodOn

Anyone else disappointed by *Piranha 3DD*?

To the Wonder's going to Venice!!!!! #GettingMyGondolaOn

Hey – I might even do some press this time.
#OnlyKiddingMotherf**kers!!!!!!!!!

About to get on plane – what do you guys think would be
best: new JK Rowling or *Threat Vector*?

I got both! I'm in premium economy: extra legroom for me,
bitches!!!! #ComplimentaryCashews

I hate Venice.

Canceling my subscription to @TimeOutLondon: 'most talk
emerges'? How many stars would you give that phrase,
fucktard?

@TimeOutLondon. Whatever. You're just jealous.

@TimeOutLondon. Brad Pitt just told me that people don't
even buy *Time Out* any more and now they give it away for
free like *Metro*.

I formally apologize to all my fans for using the word f***t**d.
I've always thought it just meant fucking idiot, altho you
probably can't even say that any more. #PCGoneMad

I really don't want this unfortunate incident to overshadow the
film. It's an easy target for journalists . . . (contd)

. . . and it's actually sort of pathetic.

Duders!!! The new trailer for *To the Wonder* drops tonight!!!!

That's the spirit! You'll get more work soon!
RT: **@BenAffleck**. As I said, I reject the notion of a pervasive hopelessness.

@BenAffleck. Dude, I was joking!

@BenAffleck. You're not the only one in the world concerned about voter apathy, Ben.

@BenAffleck. If you're so concerned about the environment why don't you fart less lol.

@BenAffleck. It's called methane, lantern head! #ReadABook

'You shall love, whether you like it or not' will not, REPEAT NOT, be used as the tagline to the new . . . (contd)

. . . Kentucky Fried Chicken campaign. #DontBelieveDumb-Rumors

Yeah I do like to love actually.

If it ain't broke don't fix it. #HellYeahVOAndLensFlare

Thanks @OlgaKurylenko – I really liked working with you too! #biased

@OlgaKurylenko. Yes you're definitely still in it! Lol.

231

@**OlgaKurylenko**. Quite a lot of skipping, yes.

@**OlgaKurylenko**. I haven't seen *Skyfall* yet – can't wait tho!

@**Eminem**. Weirdly it's out in England first then America I think. #GoFigure #BeatsMe

Just saw a lovely butterfly but I didn't have any film. #HateItWhenThatHappens

@**javierbardem**. Thanks man. It was the middle of the day, anyway. How's things in Spain? Hot, I bet.

Selected Terrence Malick Emails

In a surprising move, Terrence Malick, the camera-shy auteur, is releasing a coffee-table book of his complete Gmail correspondence, accompanied by majestic images of eagles, motivational maxims and the secret recipe for his chunky salsa dip. Herewith selected extracts.

Hey dude,
Muchos gracias for sending my ass the new Snoop Dogg joint – I didn't know you could fuckin send an album through THIN AIR!!! I'm not even gonna try to think too hard about how the computer does it!! I find it fuckin freaky sometimes. Where is the music in an iPod even comin from!!! It's like it's possessed!!! I won't have one in my pocket – it scares the shit outta me. Somethin with that much music in it should at least be heavier. Or really hot like lava.

   Anyhoo – I'm goin off on one again, I know!!! Same ol' Tel. Same ol' bullshit, ha, ha, ha!

   It's just iTunes is stressin me out, bro – it keeps asking me if I agree to terms, and I don't fuckin know. I'm not a lawyer, I just wanna listen to some beats. It's fuckin too much, dog. I'm gonna do a bucket then maybe hit the free weights for a sesh. Peace out, bitch!!!!!

PS: Yes, I DO like the Snoop Dogg Hot Pockets ad. I thought it was FUNNY!!! Plus that girl in it is fiiiiiine!!!!! Fact is, any artist's gonna get static. Haters gonna hate!

BTW, did you see *Shame*? Michael Fassbender's pecker's pretty long! It's almost half as long as mine, ha, ha, ha! But seriously – is that normal? Because I got depressed when I saw it and I couldn't really concentrate throughout the rest of the film. I think it's pretty stupid to like show some dude's massive dick at the start of a film. I mean it's not very considerate. How are you meant to enjoy the rest of the film when you've got some fuckin actor's massive length in your mind? It's fuckin sloppy directin is what it is. I mean I've never had any complaints, I just don't need to see some other fella's junk is all. I spent the whole day in the bath wondering whether there was any point comin back out.

* * *

Duder!!!!
I worked out iTunes!!!! Probably cost my ass about a hundred Gs on Apple Support, but I did it!!!!! Now it's all coooool and the gaaaaaaang. I can just computer click and get all the fresh shit I want. It's like having a big magic finger.

I love Usher. Shit y'all, that mo'fo's slick.

Nothin really happenin here. Jack Fisk made me watch *Amour* by that Haneke fuck last night. By the end I wanted to put a pillow over MY face, ha, ha, ha! Had to pop on *Bad Boys II* just to get over my downer.

PS: I guess I just like those big ol' hats. I can't wear baseball caps cos they make me look like Rob Reiner, ha, ha, ha! Respect to the brother for *Tap* tho. I wish I looked more like the main dude from *Thor*. He's fuckin handsome. I bet he gets all the chicken he wants. Oh and maybe *A Few Good Men* but not really cos I wouldn't even have watched that shit if it wasn't for Cruise. Cruise is the Mack.

234

PPS: I REALLY want to check out *Gravity*, but I hate wearin those dumb-ass glasses cos they make me look like I'm in ZZ Top. I mean my beard's not as long, but that's only cos it got stuck in the zipper of my fleece once and I cried for like an hour. I'm SERIOUS, dog! That shit HURT!!!!!!

Bullock's still fine tho. Imagine tappin that chicken in zero gravity – Clooney's so slick – do they bone in the film? SPOILER ALERT?!!! Ha, ha!

Plus I had a Nespresso the other day and it was actually okay. Why doesn't anyone ever ask ME to be in a Nespresso commercial? Guess I'm not slick enough for em, ha, ha, ha!

Actually, hold up, cousin! I just got a Russell Crowe Google Alert – Smell ya later!

S-H-H-H-H-E-E-E-E-E-I-I-I-I-I-I-I-I-I-I-I-T!!!!!!
DID YOU SEE THE TRAILER FOR *NOAH*??!!!!!!!!!!!!!!!

Your boy Crowe looks like Barry Gibb! I hope that ark comes with a mirrorball, ha, ha, ha! It was pretty ill when he sticks his sword down and the GROUND CATCHES FIRE! Doesn't he know metal is a conductor! #YouBetterBeWearingGlovesBitch

That sea looked *choppy*, cousin. I couldn't have been Noah cos I get seasick and I don't think they had those wristbands back then. Shit was tough – sometimes I'm glad I'm a contemporary metaphysical auteur and I don't have to singlehandedly repopulate the earth after a worldwide flood.

BTW, did you notice how *young* Russell Crowe's feet look? They look like a new baby's. Like they're fresh out the packet. Who's his chiropodist, dog, cos I'm gonna book an appointment!!! My hoofs are all bent up like a bag of smashed Twiglets. But then it cut to his face and he looked so tired, man. He needs a lie-in. But who am I to say – I'm always up for the dawn, motherfuckers!!!!

Ayoade's Famous Card-File System

I'll let Ayoade introduce this one . . .

From an early age I've kept a card file on every film I've ever seen. I write a brief summary followed by my critical response. When I rewatch the film, I'll update the entry with fresh impressions. How do I feel about the film now? Has it changed at all? If so, how? Have *I* changed? *How* have I changed? Have *movies* changed? *How* have movies changed? *Should* movies change? What *is* a movie, anyway? Why this *obsession* with change? And *italicising*? The cards are both aide-memoire and autobiography, a *true* 'cine-file'.
I now have over twenty-five cards. Herewith card #8.

STRICTLY BUSINESS (1991, Warner Bros)
Dir: Kevin Hooks

Bobby (Tommy Davidson), a fun-loving mailboy in a big corporation, is going nowhere fast, passed over for promotion and routinely disrespected by his boss (a spirited Sam Jackson). By contrast, his friend Waymon (Joseph C. Phillips) is a high-flyer in the same company and about to make partner.

W. wants out of his relationship with Diedre, an uptight aspirant (Anne-Marie Johnson). While on a business lunch,

W. sees the girl of his dreams in the glamorous figure of reluctant waitress/would-be club manageress Natalie (Halle Berry). *B.,* who knows *N.* through the nightclub scene, agrees to help *W.* with *N.* if *W.* will help him get him onto the trainee broker programme.

W. spends the days working on the lucrative Savoy Tower Deal and the nights attempting to woo *N.* at various clubs (a richly comic section alternates between his inexpert nocturnal forays and his increasing fatigue in the office).

Two rival businessmen, jealous of W.'s dizzying ascent, almost scupper the STD by falsifying the projections. W. rashly blames B., but the two are quickly reconciled. B. manages to source new buyers for the STD and uncover the turncoat colleagues. W. is made partner and B. gets a small office.

A condition of the STD is that the new owners allow N. to manage a nightclub on its ground floor. The film ends on the club's opening night: W., N. and (to a lesser extent) B. lost in dance.

A+ Grade.

Strictly Business fearlessly confronts race, yuppie culture and the timeless mysteries of love. Berry is introduced in one of the best tilt-up-from-high-heels-via-short-skirt-and-cleavage shots of the nineties.

Tommy Davidson's puckish Bobby is a much deeper creation than De Niro's shallow portrait of Johnny Boy in the vastly overrated *Mean Streets* (see Card #3)

2nd Viewing

Exceptional. So many great lines: 'You know what, G? You are straight-up whiter than the *whitest* white man!'

'The presentation was excellent, Waymon, but I'm concerned about those projections' – so nuanced! Every time Waymon pleases, he is also given criticism! Jungian yin-yang? You bet!

B: Am I still your trainee?
W: You know it.
B: It's you know *that.*

So cutting! So simple! *Remember* this DIRECTNESS in your own work!!

Montage of W. trying on different 'funky' clothes is masterful in its economy. A simple, repeated cut-away shot of discarded clothing options is enough to convey how long the process must have taken. When they finally hit upon an outfit that seems acceptable to both parties, *their* joy is *our* joy (in CINEMA!).

Fatal Pause: The Films That Never Were

The following first appeared in the *Week-On!* supplement special on 'Mired Movies'.

Convincing people to give you money so that you can make a film entirely on your own terms, with no guarantees as to whether they'll receive a return on their investment, is a tedious and humiliating process. Showing some puffed-up heathen a script is clearly out of the question, as is agreeing to meet the moneyed vermin. So I've taken to allowing would-be funders of my future magnum opera seventy-five seconds in a sealed room of my choosing in which they are invited to scan through a personal manifesto for the work in question. They must then destroy said napkin and transfer the agreed sums to a secure offshore account, or risk losing the opportunity of working with me FOR EVER.

I share with you one such humble treatise for a project I've been working on now for nearly twenty minutes. Any donations gratefully accepted (but not returned).

'WHAT IS LOVE? THE HADDAWAY STORY' – AN ORIGINAL ENVISIONING BASED ON THE WIKIPEDIA ENTRY

'A journey of a thousand miles begins with a single step'
Lao-tzu (604–531 BC*), *The Way of Lao-tzu*

* Before Cars?

'The real voyage of discovery consists in not seeking new landscapes but in having new eyes.'
  Marcel Proust (1871–1922), author of *The Remembrance of Things Past* and winner of the Spectacle Wearer of the Year award 1912.

THOUGHTS ABOUT A FILM ABOUT HADDAWAY: EUROLOVE

LET OUR FILM BE ABOUT LOVE, BUT NOT A 'LOVE' STORY.

FOR WHAT IS LOVE? (AS HADDAWAY SAID.)

WE MUST QUESTION EVERYTHING. EVEN HADDAWAY.

EVEN QUESTIONS?

THEREFORE: A LOVE 'STORY'? 'A' LOVE STORY? A LOVE S'TO'RY?

What?
Is?
Love?

'BABY DON'T HURT ME
DON'T HURT ME
(NO MORE)'

WHO WAS HADDAWAY? WE ALL KNOW HIM AS THE SON OF A DUTCH OCEANOGRAPHER AND A TRINIDADIAN NURSE, WHO BRIEFLY WORKED AS A CARPET SALESMAN BEFORE BECOMING ONE OF THE PIVOTAL FIGURES

IN NINETIES EURODANCE. BUT HADDAWAY IS MORE THAN THAT. HE IS, ABOVE ALL, A MAN. THIS FILM MUST FIND THAT MAN.

BUT HOW? WE FOLLOW THE PATH THAT HE GAVE US WITH HIS MUSIC!

A HADDA'PATH'? NO: A HADDA'WAY'!

BUT WHO COULD PLAY HIM? WOULD HADDAWAY BE TOO OBVIOUS A CHOICE? PERHAPS . . .

HELL'S TEETH! THIS IS GOING TO BE MORE COMPLEX THAN I THOUGHT!

POSSIBLE ACTORS: LENNY HENRY (FOR THE OLDER HADDAWAY), EWAN MCGREGOR (COULD HE DO THE ACCENT?), CHRISTOPHER PLUMMER (AS THE GHOST OF HADDAWAYS PAST).

NOTE: YOU MUST RESIST THE TEMPTATION TO OVERUSE HADDAWAY SONGS ON THE SOUNDTRACK. THAT'S EXACTLY WHAT EVERYONE WOULD EXPECT YOU TO DO! BE BRAVE, AYOADE! EVER BE BRAVE!

REMEMBER: THIS WILL BE THE FIRST FILM TO TAKE THE PHENOMENON OF EUROBEAT SERIOUSLY! ALL FANS OF HI-NRG AND EURODISCO WILL BE LOOKING TO *YOU* TO TELL *THEIR* STORY. DO NOT FAIL THEM, AYOADE! HISTORY AND EUROGROOVE WILL JUDGE YOU!

My bank details are as follows . . .

A Letter to Craig and Yasmin

My dear (soon-to-be) friends (depending on how it goes)
We are about to begin a mysterious and wonderful journey.
Not just along the M4 corridor, but to a magical place called
My Imagination. It's going to be a hell of a trip. Do you have
the correct change for the toll? (That is a light-hearted
metaphor – but you actually will need £5.40 for the Severn
Bridge as of 1 January 2009 for a Category One Vehicle.
This charge is non-refundable and will be docked from your
wages.)

I don't need to remind you how lucky you both are. I have
chosen you out of the two other people I auditioned for
Submarine to play Oliver and Jordana (we'll decide on who
plays who later), but please remember: I have kept those two
other people on the payroll AND THEY CAN REPLACE
YOU ANY TIME I WANT. Keep this in mind when you're
acting (but don't let it show in your faces and thus ruin your
acting BECAUSE THIS WILL FORCE ME TO FIRE YOU).

Inevitably, during the process of filming you will become
very attached to me. But, when the shoot ends, you will have
to leave the nest I've feathered for you and flap, squawking,
back into the real world, like the naive little chicks you are.
AND IT WILL BE FRIGHTENING WITHOUT ME. For
during your time under my majestic wing I will have been your
Everything. I will have become like God to you.

But I'm probably not God. And even though there may be
compelling evidence to the contrary, you must try to assume
that I'm not the sole Universal Life Force. However, like God,

I will have made you with mine own two hands, and for that you must be ETERNALLY GRATEFUL or a FEARFUL RECKONING will be sent unto you.

But most importantly, have fun; enjoy yourselves; and try to use the opportunity to learn from me (but DO NOT BETRAY ME by using what you've learnt on *Submarine* in any other, inevitably inferior, film roles you might get).

In fond expectation of a compliant couple of years,
Ayoade

PS: With regards to fees etc., it's really best to sort that kind of stuff out after we've completed filming. It'll only stress you out to talk about it before, and I'm sort of disappointed that you even brought it up, Craig. Also, I'd strongly advise you against getting agents/managers. These people are vampires and will suck the blood out of your tiny non-Equity little necks. We'll keep the business side of it very casual and just between you, me and my legal people.

PPS: Also – Yasmin – can you photocopy this letter and post a copy to Craig? I don't have his address any more.

Submarine **Workbook**

Doubts assault me. Is this the right story to tell? Should I have stuck with the one about the man who discovers that the spirit of his dead wife is trapped inside his uncle's dachshund? Perhaps, but it would have been difficult to get a star of any calibre to consent to the sex scenes.

I sense the crew doesn't respect me. Maybe I *do* lack concentration. But how can I concentrate when they keep towel-flicking me? Should I stop directing naked? Or should I try to stem the buying and selling of towels on set? Maybe if I allowed the crew to see the script they might feel more included in the process. But how can I show them the script when I haven't written it yet? And how can I write the script if I haven't read the book it's meant to be based on? And how can I get any time to read when I have a film to shoot? Sisyphus, I envy thee!

The part of Graham T. Purvis, the protagonist's nemesis, calls for movie-star magnetism, animal physicality and the constant underlying threat of aggression. Why didn't I cast myself? Instead I settle on Paddy Considine. Perhaps working with me will finally bring him some much-needed gravitas. He seems grateful for the video recordings I've sent him of me acting out his scenes. I hope he resists the temptation to slavishly copy my acting style. I've encouraged him to add his own touches, even to stay in character if it helps. It seems to be working.

244

Today, he punched me in the throat while I was deseeding my mid-morning kiwi. Collaboration, you are joy!

I'm finding it hard to sleep, and it's even worse at night. Must build more naps into the schedule. Apparently, the actors resent me nodding off during takes. Don't they understand how tiring and boring it is to watch them all day?

The cast stage a rebellion. I counter by staging my one-man version of *The Nutcracker*. It's so good they all start filming me on their camera phones. It's only week one. How many more ballets must I dance before they trust me?

We're nearing the end of the shoot. I'm exhausted, but I'm doing the best pirouetting of my life. My leg muscles are like ham hocks. Am worried I'm getting bottom-heavy, like a spinning top.

What do I want to say with this film? What do I want to say at all? Perhaps all I can say is, 'This is a film.' But what kind of tagline is that? Oh muse, thou art woe!

Schiess Selects

cutcutcutschiess
to me
Thanks for your telegram outlining your 'Vision' for the film (though I have to say 'Vision' puts me in mind of a team name on *The Apprentice*, particularly when you insist on capitalising it). I would suggest that the story *can* be told in under nine hours. Particularly if we remove the extended tank battle you insisted on staging.

cutcutcutschiess
to me
The extra in the back of the scene is not only looking at the camera, he's also shaking his head in despair. Can we reshoot? Also, I think he has a point.

cutcutcutschiess
to me
Please do not call me. The shrill tone of your already nasal voice is very disruptive to my work. Of course I can see why you're worried. If I were you, I would've probably committed suicide by now. But please don't take your understandable concerns about your total lack of talent (or 'Vision') out on me. I don't know 'what the hell we can do about it' either.

cutcutcutschiess
to me
An improvement. Bravo! I hear you were off sick and the

assistant director took over for the day. Perhaps a fortuitous event that points to a better working method?

cutcutcutschiess
to me
Good footage this week. Some of the performances are wonderful. But are you able to stop playing the French horn while you're watching at the monitor? It's making it hard to get any rhythm to the dialogue. And by the way, your C-natural is flat. I think you may be using too much bottom lip.

cutcutcutschiess
to me
The tone is coming together. The balance of romance and regret could really work. Which is why I wonder whether we need that dream sequence with the spaceship crewed by three-breasted aliens. I know it's one of your favourite scenes, but the budgetary constraints really show. Despite the art department working miracles, a meat counter at a Morrisons is never going to look like the bridge of a star-fighter. At the very least can we trim down the pillow fight on the flight deck? The sound of the crew clapping along doesn't help the already creepy feel.

cutcutcutschiess
to me
Do you definitely see this as a feature? I think there *may* be enough material for a relatively worthwhile short.

Danny Deville on *The Double*

DannytotheD
to me

Hey I can't believe you're doing a new film – didn't anyone see the last one?! But seriously, first films are hard so don't be too rough on yourself. I'm told it definitely had its moments. This is just to say hey and best of luck and here's hoping people want to go see this one for some reason.

Just a brief thought – does it have to be called THE DOUBLE? I feel that Richard Gere and Topher Grace made a pretty interesting film called THE DOUBLE back in '11 about a retired CIA operative who's paired with a young FBI rookie to unravel the mystery of a senator's untimely demise. All signs point to the Ruskies, and Gere's spent his whole life going toe to toe with Reds. But the young punk has his own ideas about how to conduct the investigation. Frankly, it blew me away and I think it's a little cocky, not to mention disrespectful, to give your movie the same name. Why don't you just call it JAWS, you fuckin illiterate?

Okay, so my hot assistant just told me your film is based on a book that was apparently written 'before' 2011. But let me ask you this. Do you really think it's a good idea to be basing films on books written before 2011? Don't you want to be relevant? And do you really want to be associated with a book written by a Russian?! A Russian who didn't even have the goddamn courtesy to avoid titular overlap with a remarkable late-period piece by Richard Gere?

Also, if I've learned anything in Hollywood it's Avoid

Dostoevsky Like Dairy (ADLD). No one wants to wade through the ravings of some commie epileptic who, by the way, was only five foot two.

Do you know how many successful films have been made out of Dostoevsky novels? How's about NOT EVEN CLOSE TO ONE SUCCESSFUL FILM. And you had to choose ONE OF HIS LEAST SUCCESSFUL NOVELS. A novel that even that seizure-throwing son of a Pinsk wasn't happy with! Are you trying to die? Are you literally trying to die in this business? Do you realize how hard it is to stay awake if you even say the name Dostoevsky? If I say that name out loud my eyes glaze over – it's like seeing about ten billion sheep gently gavotte over a breeze-blown hedge at dusk. It's like when I started smoking Valium. It's like watching a silent film that isn't THE ARTIST.

Look – it's up to you, but I'm betting there isn't even one scene in that book where the hero power-slides under a mechanically closing door. And that saddens the shit out of me.

Anyway, just have a think about it and whether you want to have any work in five years' time or whether you'd rather be (distantly) remembered as the maker of a couple of curios.

See ya!

DannytotheD
to me
So I watched some of your interviews for your last thing, and after I got my hot assistant to resuscitate me I thought I'd send you some pointers on promoting your DOUBLE movie after you get through all that boring shit of filming it and putting all the footage in a row or whatever the hell you guys do during the 'edit' (why don't you just shoot the stuff you *need*!??? Then you wouldn't need to cut so much to get it to the right length!).

Okay – here goes.

Try to avoid any talk of the film being about 'loneliness'.
Do you know what's lonely? Being the only person at the
premiere of your goddamn movie because everyone heard
you just made a film about loneliness. Do you know what
Avatar is about? Me neither, but it sure as Satan ain't about
loneliness. If you have to use a noun, how about 'horniness'?
Loneliness is individual. Horniness is universal. At its core,
this is a film about a fun, horny guy trying to get laid, right?

Don't mention Dostoevsky. The man is no JK Rowling. And,
as I've mentioned before, he's Russian.

Try and emphasize how short the film is. Having seen some
of it, I think this could be a key selling point.

This time, could you try and at least sound like you're not
flat-out ashamed to be associated with the film? It doesn't
sound like modesty, by the way. You sound like you're twelve.
A young twelve. A very young twelve-year-old who ought to
know better. The kind of twelve-year-old I'd shout at. And
his parents would be like, We probably shouldn't be saying
this, but we're pleased you shouted at him. He's a hateful
disappointment.

Note for TV interviews: stop shifting your weight between
your legs – you look like you're trying to stand up in a dingy.
And maintain eye contact. Eye contact is one of the few
things that distinguish us from Mexicans.

An observation: although your hair is large, your actual
head is small. That won't fly in Hollywood. Here everyone
has giant domes. Little people with big heads: that's the LA
way. Cranial enlargement is a little out of your price range so
I suggest you shrink your body. You can cut out fluids for a
week if you don't move much.

And while we're on the subject of weight, you look like the
'before' photograph in a Slim Fast commercial . . . how can

you stand to eat so much? You live in England. Why not try the DeVille Diet:

Breakfast
Half a cup of kale, a quarter cup of soy, two steamed broccoli stems. Drink: 50ml water

Lunch
Half a cup of kale, one cup of soy, one steamed broccoli stem. Drink: 30ml soy milk or 50ml water.

Dinner
Half a cup of kale, a cup of soy/millet mix, two or three walnuts. Drink: 20ml low-sodium tomato-juice substitute.

And don't worry if you find yourself crying for periods of up to four hours – that's completely normal for this type of cleanse.

Finally – not a PR thing – but have you thought about using some rap on the soundtrack? We're repping some exciting talent, many of whom might be up for parole soon.

DannytotheD
to me
So I got the artwork concepts for your 'film' and I'm going to get right to it: I think it's a HUGE fucking mistake not having a poster with the two guys back to back. It'd be like doing the one-sheet for *Twins* and not having DeVito lean up against Schwarzenegger. It's called THE DOUBLE, dumbo, not THE SINGLE, stupid. If it were THE SINGLE, the poster would be a dude peering over a pair of Ray-Bans while a hot girl loosens his tie.

I cannot overstress this, so I'll repeat: not having some kind of a B2B poster pose for a movie of this kind is not only INSANITY, it's an act of ARTISTIC COWARDICE.

As a cineaste, I presume you're familiar with the work of Matthew McConaughey. This guy won't even *be* on a trade ad unless he's at an angle.* I refer you to his inclines on the FAILURE TO LAUNCH and HOW TO LOSE A GUY IN 10 DAYS posters, two classics of the form. But don't let their unbeatable perfection depress you, the great thing about the B2BPP is that there are always ways to make it fresh and relevant, even with a film as boring as yours. Let me throw some ideas at you. Close your eyes, picture the poster, and read on.

Title: THE DOUBLE (perhaps it could be in a type that's sort of 'off', like 'doubled' in some way or maybe just neon). Below is our central image of the Double Guys. One guy is pointing his thumb at the other guy. Or one guy could grab the other guy's tie. Or one could look at his watch while the other makes a hand gesture. I know I'm literally making this up while I'm on a conference call with McG, and maybe it's this new muscle cream I'm drinking, but I'm really pumped, concept-wise.

Yes! One guy grabs the other guy's ass while he does an expression like 'WTF?!' That's it. It's fun but it's also edgy. These two guys aren't afraid to get close. We might get a little BROKEBACK buck ($178 million worldwide on a $14 million production budget – and I don't know why it cost even that much – all you needed were a couple of Stetsons and a tent). I know it's just a seed at the moment, but sometimes seeds grow into mountains. Or is the expression sometimes

* Ayoade's agent was characteristically behind the curve on the McConaissance. However, I contend that McC's best work *is* in the early 'funny' films, and the new 'serious' ones where he makes weird sounds and takes a long time to exhale cigarette smoke are to be endured and not enjoyed, and I, for one, am on full McConaboycott until he gets back to laughing good-naturedly and taking his top off.

252

seeds grow *on* mountains? But why would that even be an expression? Who cares *where* seeds grow as long as they're happy, right?

I know what you're going to say: what's the point in having a poster if Matthew McConaughey isn't on it? It's called growing a pair. Plenty of movies get released without Matthew McConaughey in them, and a lot of them do pretty well. Not having Matthew McConaughey on your poster just forces you to be more creative.

BTW, have you thought any more about changing the title to DOUBLE GUYS?

The Cutting Room

In which Ayoade addresses an actor left on the cutting-room floor.

Dearest 'X',

In my already-too-long life I've had to write innumerable difficult letters. Many have dealt with issues involving Southwark council. The few remaining others have tackled injustice of a different sort. A 'lost' item of pyjama-wear at a dry cleaner's staffed by white people; a spat over the cost of an unnecessary colonoscopy; a colleague's poorly reasoned refusal to remove his laptop case from my flat; a bitter feud with a pescetarian as to whether Pascal was, in general, a betting man. But none has been as hard as this.

As you know, I'm a tremendous fan of your work as an actor. Your exploration of 'Angry Chicken Store Owner' in *Jerkin' n' Jammin'* has long secured your place in my personal pantheon, but it was your breakout role as 'Second Angry Guy' in *This Is Why We Say What We Say* that brought me to tears. And not just of fatigue.

I was delighted that you agreed to board my production of *The Double*, even though *The Double* is a film and not a ship. Far too long had you been stereotyped as an angry terrorist in projects that were beneath your capabilities. This would be an opportunity for you to reclaim your rightful title as the 'Slovenian Vin Diesel'.

Yes, our rehearsals were tense and unnecessarily physical.

Yes, you always smelt of Tia Maria. Yes, your fierce and oft-proffered bear hugs lasted several hours. Yes, you fell asleep if we closed the window. But for a brief moment, at around 2.00 a.m. if you could still stand, you were vibrant. Like a fully mature stag glistening with dew, fresh from the chase, flanks pulsing with glorious majesty. And if we were filming at that moment, I was one happy half-Norwegian.

Which brings me to the good news:

Your performance as 'Angry Tramp' is peerless. You brought nuance and truth to a role that, in less masterful hands, might have flirted with cliché. But you made him sing. Literally, in several unusable takes. Your insistence that 'Angry Tramp' hum the entire Beatles back catalogue has meant the film has spent several months mired in costly clearance issues. But enough of remortgaging my house.

Which brings me to the bad news:

We had to cut your performance. It was simply too *powerful* for the film to take. Maybe it's something to do with how loud you speak. Maybe it's the amount of phlegm you produce (and expel) in scene work. Or maybe it's because the film just felt very boring when you were in it. But let us not dwell on technical talk, for you and I are dreamers.

Let us not feel shame, my fellow traveller, for you have made the cutting-room floor a new Valhalla. I offer this email not as an apologia but as a congratulata. For it is by YOUR magnificent standard that all future deleted scenes will be judged.

(BTW, do you still want to be credited as 'X' in the film or would you rather use a pseudonym?)

Making the Grade:
A Grading Diary

NOTE TO READERS: Digital intermediate is a motion-picture grading process that involves digitising 35mm film and manipulating the colour/image. For me, 'DI' is one of the most thrilling parts of this business called show. What could be more satisfying than spending up to three weeks in a lightless room making increasingly indiscernible colour adjustments while your retinas scream for relief. Terrified that I wouldn't remember how it felt to be this alive, I decided to document my daily joy . . .

DOUBLE TIME: MAKING *THE DOUBLE* – A DI-ARY

– What a day! It definitely feels like the warm tones at the start are going to work. The only thing to watch is that the actors' faces don't get too red. I guess putting in a little green might help. Still, it's early days, and we'll just try and do a broad-strokes pass before zeroing in on the detail. I hope fifteen days is enough time!

– Did a nice cool-blue look for some of the exterior scenes. I guess the trick was not to make the images too 'blocky' and to ensure that there was still detail within the blue. Before I knew it, three days had gone!

– Spent quite a bit of time making sure that the extra cyan in the exterior scenes didn't make the lead actor's complexion overly pinkish (not that his complexion is overly pinkish in real life – it's just a by-product of globally adding in cyan!). I hope we succeeded!

– Sometimes it seems that all that's needed is a little extra contrast! Haven't seen daylight for a good while now!

– Best Monday I've had for a week! We're providing nice contrast without crushing the blacks. I think it's going to turn out to be a really dynamic grade! I'm so happy with the interplay of all the colours that it makes no sense at all why I sometimes wake up crying.

– Is it just me or does red look quite like orange?

– How many weeks can you leave between showers? I guess as long as you're able to put up with the itchiness, it's your call. No one comes too close to me anyway and it's been a while since I've hugged someone or even got close enough to shake anyone's hand. I tend to stick to the mini-wave or half-bow. In any case, I think it'd be weird to still have friends at thirty-six.

– Can't wait to see how well these infinitesimal alterations of hue will translate to YouTube! Or the intermittent cubism of Netflix!

– Not long now before *Ender's Game* drops. That shit looks dope.

– Green is stupid.

– I know some people say that if you stop using shampoo your hair starts to clean itself, but that can't be right, can it? I mean, if not from me, where else is this smell of rotting meat coming from?

– I prefer looking at my foot than looking at this film. Is that a bad sign or do I just have a great-looking foot?

Double F.A.Q.

How was directing *The Double*?
It was all shot at night, so I was able to direct as a
werewolf, which in turn meant I spent less time agonising
about my outfits. I quickly formulated my new look: cut-
off denim shorts teamed with a ripped-open flannel shirt.
Sometimes I'd sport a sweatband and ride on top of cars
(or am I just misremembering *Teen Wolf*?).

How did you find the Dostoevsky novella?
It was Avi Korine's idea. Everything I've read of
Dostoevsky is alarmingly brilliant and unique. I think if
he'd been alive now he could've scripted *Keeping Up with
the Kardashians*. He's that good. We just feel lucky we
were born so long after him that we were able to profit
from his ideas without encountering any legal problems,
but not so long that we became embroiled in a future
apocalyptic eco-war that rendered all films a trivial
irrelevance when weighed against the struggle for our
planet's survival.

**Why is the topic of a doppelgänger ripe for exploration in
film?**
1. The actor has to do twice the amount of work for the
same fee.
2. Ripeness just makes me want to explore, especially
in film. I guess I just love topics, and that combined
with the ripeness made the whole idea irresistible. And I

258

can't resist the irresistible as a direct consequence of that word's definition! And I've always loved doppelgängers! And the idea of cinematically combining that with a topic was just so exciting!!

Why were Jesse and Mia right for the cast?
They're two of the best actors in the world; they are a pleasure to be around; and they're surprisingly tolerant of my acrid body odour. Jesse's one of those rare actors who *thrives* on sarcastic eye-rolls.

What kind of tone were you aiming for?
I like things that are funny and frightening. Sort of the opposite of *Scary Movie*. I always have a selection of tuning forks in my director's pouch. I will sound one before each take and say, '*That's* it. This is our truth today. D-sharp.'

How was it working with Terry Gilliam on the look of the film?
He was my art director on *The Need for (A Tad More) Speed* pre-viz sessions and we just see things the exact same way, so it made sense to use him as a consultant on every decision I made.

What's next for you?
I'm hoping to do more and more interviews. Eventually, I'd like to see the interviews replace the directing because I'm becoming increasingly frustrated during the gaps between junkets. The prospect of needing to make a whole film before a stranger tapes my thoughtless utterances (and uses them as the basis for a speculative, semi-hostile character portrait) makes me very sad.

259

An Open Letter to the Press

Reviewing a film is one of the most exhausting things in the world. You have to show up someplace, watch something, and then write an essay on whether you think anyone else ought to go through the same ordeal. And then, after every sentient organ you possess is quivering from the sheer exertion of it all, you'll probably have to think up some kind of pun as the title. Just when you've given everything, just as The Man has squeezed the lemon dry, He starts to scrape at your very zest.

So pun you must, lest your beloved reader be left without a wry primer for your distilled truth. A truth for which you've sweated soul juice: a precious, vibrant juice whose molecules thrum with integrity.

And, with each year that passes, you watch mournfully as more and more great puns are used up, tossed aside like squelchy grapes, leading you, the diligent reviewer, contorted by your own perfectionism, into ever more desperate attempts at wordplay.

Well, fear not, noble foe. Herewith fresh arrows for your quiver.

PUNS FOR USE W/R/T *THE DOUBLE*, RICHARD AYOADE'S SOPHOMORIC MISFIRE

Seeing Double A basic pun. Nothing special, but a useful first port of call.

Double Vision Another workaday pun, but a little more layered, with a nice nod to *Chuckle Vision*, the children's slapstick comedy series starring Paul and Barry Chuckle.

Double Trouble A fine pun. Good for a more generic piece where you're not sure if the reviewer has seen the film or not.

Double Impact A decent pun. Provides a good opportunity to discuss the work with reference to the much-loved Van Damme actioner.

Double or Quits? A fun, edgy pun. Especially good if your review is thirty words or less. Cinema is a time-hungry activity, and you have to make sure that the movie-goer is consuming the correct content.

Double Dip The thinking man's pun. Great for a slating AND can tackle broader economic themes.

Double Feature A classic, lovely pun. Elegant and uninflected, it also allows you to review another film within the same piece.

Double Entry A risky pun. The reader's tendency for baseness might scupper your clever reference to the production's fraudulent book-keeping.

Double Bath Allows you to review the film within the context of baths, whether it is the experience of watching the film from a bath, just after a bath, or even in the city of Bath.

Double Bass A good pun for a piece on the film's

composer, especially if your article is focused on the low-frequency spectrum of the score.

I'm Forever Blowing Doubles A somewhat desperate pun for tabloid use only. Would only really be relevant in the event that Jesse Eisenberg becomes enmeshed in a Hugh Grant/Divine Brown situation.

Double and Squeak Difficult to know how readily this pun could be employed. Perhaps better as a photo caption. Would particularly work if the photo were of a cast member eating bubble and squeak.

Double and Strife A brilliant pun.

A Letter to a Young Director

In which Ayoade responds to a would-be *metteur en scène*.

Dear Friend,

I was deeply moved by your letter because in it I saw myself as a young man. And not just because you'd included a picture of me with the eyes cut out and 'WHY MUST YOU INSIST ON LIVING, YOU TALENTLESS INSECT??' inked onto my forehead. No, I sensed in you a hunger, an earnest desire to learn about the craft. A fiery desire I share and continue to waft daily. A flame that sparked in my infant breast and kindled through days spent alone in a humble Odeon nestled in the Dreamfields of Ipswich (oh Suffolk's neglected jewel!). An inferno made incandescent by the bravura of *Herbie Goes Bananas* and other towering *meisterworks* of that Golden Age that was early-eighties US cinema. Though come to think of it, why was I being left unattended at the age of three? But perhaps that's a matter for another letter . . .

I, like you, *mon brave*, wanted to create films that would dazzle audiences just as *Herbie Goes Bananas* had dazzled me (the sequence where Paco disguises Herbie as a taxi is among the most mesmeric in all motion pictures). But how could I join such vaunted company? I thought of writing to the director and asking him how he set about constructing the precise *mise en scène* of the fourth in the series starring the charismatic Volkswagen racing Beetle, but the fear of hubris forbade me. Timidity does not seem to be your weakness, though, as your frequent letters, postcards and suspect packages attest. Your impatience is palpable. What, maestro (you seem to be saying underneath it all), is the secret to great directing? Herewith some suggestions:

1. Pick out an outfit. You're the head of a team and should be easily identifiable. I sport a canary-yellow boiler suit teamed with a tan leather flight jacket and a hard hat. It's stylish, authoritative and highly visible. In it I feel I can direct the heck out of anything: from a Fish-Out-of-Water Workplace-Based Comedy to an Older-Man-in-Peril Invasion Epic.

2. Conserve your energy. Sometimes it's better for everyone if you direct from your hammock. I've always said: if you're not feeling relaxed, you're not in a hammock.

3. Listen. Listen. Listen. Or just Listen (if you paid attention the first time).

4. Only use drugs to reward yourself for a job well done, not as a crutch.

5. Decide what kind of beard you want.*

The rest is up to you. You certainly possess the requisite overconfidence, rage and unjustified self-pity of a director; now all you need is the funding to make those adolescent revenge fantasies a reality. May fortune favour you! I must take my leave now, in compliance with the expectations of

* #everydaysexism.

the epistolary genre. Namely: wrap it up pronto, Tonto. Be brave, my friend! And I hope you appreciate that many of the suggestions you've made in your letters to me are not ones I am physically able to enact.

Ever,

Ayoade

'Three Thousand Dreams Snatched from the Sky': A Tribute to Karl-Anders Von Boten

The following article first appeared in *The Really Real Reel Review for Tablet Devices* under the title 'The Death of the Auteur (In Association with Sodastream)'.

This week, the great cineaste – and my mentor – Karl-Anders Von Boten (*The Debasement of Jakob*) passed away.

By the age of eight, Karl-Anders had become an outstanding athlete, logician and flautist, as well as being a very good dry cleaner. But dry cleaning's loss became cinema's gain when a grateful customer gave him a film camera as a thank-you for getting ground-in egg yolk out of a cream safari jacket.

KAVB completed his debut short (*An Anguish*) in a mere seven years. Its haunting narrative about a pre-adolescent shop owner trapped in the dry-cleaning business still resonates today. He would spend a lifetime exploring and re-exploring these themes.

I had the pleasure of working with the great man in his later years. The 'Von-ster' was still wrestling with his six-part cycle of trilogies set in a filthy world of warring, ineffective dry cleaners. He needed a fresh perspective: a collaborator, a friend, a fellow adventurer who despised stains as much as he did. The day after the money had been securely transferred to my bank and my expenses had been negotiated, we sat down to write.

266

Von Boten didn't like to hold a pen. Rather he would shout out notes whilst pelting me with nectarines. Writing proceeded slowly. Five, maybe six words a day was all I could manage, so intense was the barrage. The final films were already so vivid in his head that I imagine the frustration of waiting for someone else to plough through the trivial banalities of characterisation, dialogue and writing the entire plot from scratch must have been very tiring for him. He would regularly say, in his playful manner, that he couldn't decide what he hated more: the cinema or having to look at me. We soon worked out a system: he would bombard me with guavas for three hours at the start of the day, we'd eat lunch in bitter silence, and then I would write during the afternoon while he napped.

Sadly, it was during one of those naps that he shot himself. I ran as fast as my bruised body would allow, fell to my (agonised) knees and cradled the truncated auteur. Incredibly, he was still alive. His eyes, the eyes that had framed so many marvellous tableaux, were fixed on me. Some words formed on his lips, his *last* words: 'It's not really *dry* cleaning. It's just non-water based . . .' Then he struck me with an unripe pawpaw. By the time I regained consciousness he was dead.

I wept. Tears of acrid grief poured onto my prized silk ruff (a gift from Ron Howard). Which became stained. So I had to go and take the item to a . . . I dare not write the words! How right Karl-Anders was! It is indeed the *only* story to tell!

Filmy Feelings:
An Essay on Film and Feeling

The following piece, written as a shooting script, first appeared as a foreword to the now-out-of-print *Ayoade: The Films of My Life*. It is also available in *The Selected Forewords of Richard Ayoade*.

Fade in.

INT. NIGHT — SOMEWHERE

Our camera TRACKS into the face of AYOADE, his masculine curls caressed by a moonlight gust.

We hear his inner monologue.

> AYOADE (V.O.)
> I've lived in film, for film and through film; I've lived by film and to buy film; I've bought film and I've bought into film; I've been in film (for *The Watch is* technically a film); film has been in me (and had to be removed under local anaesthetic).
>
> I've sold film (on eBay); I've been sold into (one or two) films (for Equity minimum).
>
> I've seen the film *Grease*; I've seen a film of grease; I've yet to see a film in Greece or while being greased. I've cried at films, I've cried out for films, I've wept in Chicken Cottage.

Music swells.

I've viewed blockbusters; I've eschewed Blockbusters (now I lament the demise of independent rental outlets while simultaneously reaping the benefits of Internet shopping and home delivery but occasionally cursing the attendant stress and inconvenience of missing deliveries and having to collect them from a depot – I mean, I think sometimes they just come out with the cards and aren't even carrying the packages).

Rain lashes down, thunder sounds, the camera cranes up, a dizzying exhortation to the heavens (budget permitting. Otherwise camera ZOOMS; the weather remains pleasant.)

I cling to film and I've used cling film (though I prefer the crunch of BacoFoil); film is in my heart, film is in my veins (which is one of the reasons why I can't safely give blood) and, in recent years, I've obtained almost enough funding to make films to a semi-professional level.

Highlights of said work. A Dizzying Flourish. The Screen Burns out from the INTENSITY.

FULL FRAME RED. We slowly mix through to reveal the sleeping face of Ayoade. Bloody R.E.M.?*

* Certain Ayoade scholars have suggested that this looks like a covert swipe at Stipe and co. But actually Ayoade has expressed gratitude that someone as nasal as Stipe managed to achieve mainstream success, thus paving the way for Ayoade's adenoidal buzz.

This book is about films. My films, their films, your films, *our* films.*

Filming films. Filmy films. Film films.

Film.

Just film.

Nothing else.

Except film.

It's also a book. And therefore, in some sense, is about books, or at least forms part of the continuing discussion about what is a book (one of my favourite continuing discussions), but that shouldn't get in the way of our main purpose here, which is . . .

We cut to –

* Notwithstanding, the copyright of this book resides with the author.

Sample Diary Entry

In which we get a sense of Ayoade's mindscape during this trying period.

23 MAY

Met with Unnamed Funding Body about my Unnamed Project.* Was difficult to hear myself think over sound of buzzing, though I can't remember whether thinking makes a sound. A high-ranking space midge (maybe a general, tricky to be definite) picked at carrion throughout. Fluffed the pitch – realised I was essentially just recapping the plot to an old *Star Trek* episode.** Towards the end of the meeting a junior-ranking female sand

---

* Both pseudonymous.
** Which would have at least possessed more originality than the film *Argo*. Having viewed this assault on my human purpose, I wrote to the Islamic Republic of Iran, asking whether it would join me in a lawsuit against the film. Herewith my chief contentions:

1. That the idea of Ben Affleck playing someone who could pass as a filmmaker is so ludicrous as to be offensive.
2. That much of the wig, glasses and moustache work in *Argo* is route-one seventies wig, glasses and moustache work, and is therefore offensive.
3. That the subplot of Hero as Absentee Father Redeemed by His Adherence to a Noble and/or Dangerous Cause was trite and clichéd even at the time of the Iranian hostage crisis.
4. That having Philip Baker Hall in a film and only using him in one scene is offensive.
5. That *Argo* winning the Academy Award for Best Picture when *The Master* wasn't even nominated is offensive (*contd*).

271

gnat brought me a sandwich for my lunch and said that I could have another if I wanted but I said that I was full and anyway did I look like the kind of person who ate several sandwiches in a row like some kind of fat fuck but I actually did want another sandwich because the one she brought looked pretty small but by that stage it was a matter of fucking principle so I fired her and

6. That Ben Affleck's blink rate is at so high a frequency that it could cause epilepsy in Iranians unused to Western acting of this type and, as such, is offensive.

7. That Steadicam is overused in the film and that the Steadicam moves themselves often lack motivation, thus violating Jean-Luc Godard's dictum that 'a tracking shot is a moral issue', and that such a violation is offensive to the Republic of Iran.

8. That Alan Arkin did better work in *Santa Clause 3: The Escape Clause*.

9. That the people of Iran would rather have seen the actual science-fiction-film version of *Argo*, as it looked quite good from the storyboards, without prejudice to the fact that using storyboards in a title sequence (unless it's a documentary about the making of A-ha's 'Take on Me' music video) is offensive.

10. That the idea that the joke about the WGA being 'more scary' than the ayatollah could even be considered a joke is offensive both to Iran and to the concept of jokes.

11. That, now, normal air travel is considerably more stressful than it was depicted in *Argo*, and at least back then you could take a packed lunch on a plane or even a thermos if you wanted and no one could stop you.

12. That having a scene where PERSON 1 calls PERSON 2 in order to obtain vital information and having the camera track in to a ringing phone and showing that there's no one around to pick up the ringing phone and then cutting to PERSON 2 (who ought to be picking up the Tracked-into-Phone) not being able to get to the Tracked-into-Phone for some bullshit reason and then cutting back to PERSON 1 waiting for PERSON 2 to pick up the Still-Ringing-and-Tracked-into-Phone and then pushing into PERSON 1 looking like he's just about ready to give up and cradle the receiver before, at the crucial moment, PERSON 2 picks up and answers just in time is offensive.

13. That *Argo* essentially rips off, but isn't as good as, any of the films in the *Delta Force* trilogy.

she said she didn't work for me and that she was actually working for the people who I was taking the meeting with (she used the word 'people', which must have
been some kind of code word for 'space midges') and I
said if you're so in love with them why don't you give
THEM the sandwiches and frankly how can a bunch of
gnats be expected to run a competent production company and I was so fucking angry that I threw the tiny
sandwich on the floor so I had to go to Prêt à Manger
and I bought a Prêt's Nuts About Christmas sandwich
because the Prêt's Christmas Lunch ones had sold out
because it was already three by then but I also did think
it was a funny name for a sandwich and anyway I was
kind of tired and didn't want to argue too much with
the people there about why didn't they make sure that
they had enough sandwiches in the place given that's
their sole fucking job and were they trying to fuck me or
something but I think I'd eaten too many satsumas earlier and my stomach felt kind of acidy or maybe it was
the coffee so I leaned against the counter for a while and
tried to have an idea but then they had to close the shop.

A New Manifesto for F(i)lm

The following first appeared in *Movies, Movies, Movies!!!!*

When I start a new piece of work, I always try to set myself rules. I feast on principles, aphorisms and maxims. Brilliant *pensées* that act as a guiding light for any writer/director/sitcom actor in this messed up *monde*. For years I have kept the following cards on my bunker wall:

Do Not Confuse the Eye with the Ear, Especially
When Putting on Glasses.

Abolish All Distance Between Yourself and the Actors,
Except When They're Getting Changed.

Patience Is Not Only Not a Virtue, It Also
Slows Everything Down.

In Film: Soul Should Be Made Flesh. In Life:
Sole Should Be Made Fresh.

But as I circle an exciting new film project (the details of which I can't disclose, except that it will encompass both tap dancing and Victorian naval policy), I feel the need to provide myself with even tighter strictures. If you permit, I shall share them with you now:

274

1. No more actors. They are all cowards. From now on just use fishermen and cobblers.
2. Record no sounds that could be described as 'pre-existing'. Use only sounds the human ear has never heard before! Do not listen to the soundtrack of the film until it has been released!
3. No more lunch. It weakens the intellect.
4. No more cameras. We must find a new way! I propose using 'memory stone' to record images. I will only exhibit my films to wizards.
5. No ego (or Eno).
6. Crew should number no more than two people and be NON-PROFESSIONALS (either two fishermen or two cobblers or one of each).
7. The image must not include the idea of IMAGE, except when it is an image of an idea of Image or an image of an Idea (in which case, it may require special lighting, which is NOT ALLOWED).
8. The film must not be edited.
9. The film must have no title.
10. The film must not be a film.

I think we must all stand by these statements both as filmmakers and as audiences (except number 3 – I think I was just full up when I wrote it).

Don't you feel alive to the new possibilities?! We need a New Cinema! One without cameras or actors or titles or crew or editing or films or Brian Eno! No more stories! No more authorship! We must remove the idea of 'I' from Films! Let there be Flm! I will lead you!

Manifesto Update: The Flm-ifesto has proved unworkable. Who else could produce a synth-based score for a story about tap-dancing Victorian admirals starring Colin Firth?

pROject-OR Short Film

The following is a transcription of a short film that first appeared in the e-zine *pROject-OR*. The film, written and directed by Ayoade, was a response to the following challenge:

1. Envision a short film that captures the process of Creation, then film that envision. Or don't film it, whichever feels more true.
2. The film, should you film it, must be no longer than the length, in metres, of your longest toe.
3. The film must contain James Franco (even if you don't film it).

The piece that Ayoade birthed comprised an imagistic triptych:

1. Black-and-white camera-phone clips of Ayoade hula-hooping naked apart from one moon boot – back fat quivering in the dawn – under the influence of Benylin.
2. Slowed-down Super 8 film of a Jack Russell dry-humping a map of the Netherlands.
3. The film *Mr Popper's Penguins* playing on an iPad lodged in an Antarctic ice shelf, while indigenous penguins occasionally shimmy up and scan the footage with weary dejection at their continued comic misrepresentation.

IMAGES: A SHORT JOINT BY AYOADE
in association with SAINSBURY'S LOCAL

Words by Ayoade; music by Johnny Borrell; guitar by David Gilmour.

Voice . . . . . . Franco

                        VOICE
It starts with an image.
    An image that makes your heart quicken, your breath shallow, your legs fan out.

            OVER-70S MALE-VOICE CHOIR
Images.

                        VOICE
They haunt me – they caress me – they're rude to me – they won't pick me up from the airport.

                  ANNIE LENNOX
Images.

                        VOICE
They tempt me – they cheat me – they confound me – they make remarks.

                  BORIS JOHNSON
                  (alone on a tandem)
Images.

VOICE

Two lovers argue – the man lunges forward – his pyjama bottoms fall down – the molecular degeneration of the elastic in his nightwear a metaphor for their marital collapse.

ALAIN DE BOTTON
(wet and prone on a mini-catamaran)
Images.

VOICE

A cat – paw pressed on the wing of a struggling pigeon – whispers something undermining into the crepuscular light.

JAMIE HINCE FROM THE KILLS
Images.

VOICE

A forty-something sitcom writer's face floods with joy as he receives an e-vite to a leading publication's Hot 500 nomination announcement pre-party.

A WELL-KNOWN SIGN-LANGUAGE INTERPRETER
(hands tied behind her back)
Images.

VOICE

An abandoned shopping trolley meanders mournfully through an estate peopled with ruffians who might never have the chance to see *The Bitter Tears of Petra von Kant* decently projected.

MICHAEL FASSBENDER
(scoring a rolled joint of pork)

Images.

VOICE

A large DIY superstore is deserted. Could this be the apocalypse – or is there another strange reason why it's not open?

A PROMINENT CLIMATE-CHANGE DENIER
(power-hosing his patio)

Images.

VOICE

A lunar landscape of macchiato froth disintegrates at the base of a plum demitasse. The imbiber raises her head – a look of sadness? Or has she had too much Fair Trade lemon loaf?

VERNON KAY
(gaffer-taping Pedro Almodóvar to a daybed)

Im-a-ges.

VOICE

We see something true.

Fade to black . . .

What does it look like . . .?

We hear the following in the darkness.

279

MICHAEL HANEKE

Das Ende . . .

JEAN-LUC GODARD

. . . des images?

ANNIE LENNOX

WHY?!

Dave Gilmour solo improv . . .

A Letter to an Actress

Dear Name Withheld*

I write to you as a great fan of your work. I've followed your entire career with keen interest ever since I saw you in that bleach commercial. When you walked back into the toilet and delighted (is 'bathed' too loaded a term?!) in that lemon-fresh, germ-free aroma, I knew I was faced with a young woman of savage complexity and uncompromising grace. And she could handle a parrot like a pro! I would sit glued to the television just for a chance to see that commercial again and glimpse once more that simple moment of truth. But enough about toilet bleach, let's talk about you.

I don't know if you've read the script I sent but if you haven't (and perhaps you shouldn't before you decide whether to take on this part) please don't be swayed by some of the very vicious and unfair things people have been saying about it. As far as I'm concerned *Robot Cop* has a completely different tone, sensibility and (much lower) budget to *RoboCop*, and I think comparisons between the two are not going to help anyone (least of all me). Let's settle the legal proceedings and *then* we can speculate about whether it's 'morally and artistically bankrupt'. No one sued Darren Aronofsky for doing a ballet version of *Showgirls*, and I doubt Verhoeven wants to battle this out in the courts any more now than he did then. Let's just focus on our job as storytellers.

* Presumably a pseudonym?

The role of CYBORG BABE 2 is complex, and one only an actress of your considerable gifts could handle. By the way, what weight are you at the moment? Because I know you tend to fluctuate. I only ask because we've already made the suit to fit Barbara Windsor, but to be honest I'm glad she was double-booked, and you really weren't our 'twelfth choice' – we just didn't think of you straight away. But now that we have thought of you, you're our absolute first and only choice, unless you're busy or turn it down or cost too much.

Just to warn you, though – there is partial nudity – but just on your right side – you won't have to go the full Fassbender. The left side will be covered up by circuitry, a mini-plasma screen and your pleasure dock (by the way, have you noticed that Michael Fassbender always looks like he's in the early stages of a transformation scene in a werewolf movie? I think it's the paleness of the eyes).

You'll also get the chance to work with Ross Kemp, if we can get in contact with him and he accepts the part. Kemp would play a half-blind, sex-addicted, transgender jockey from the future who fuses himself with his horse (and subsequently becomes embroiled in a protracted dispute with the Jockeys Association for trying to mount a competitor during a race).

Please call me if you want clarification on anything to do with this project, or even if you just want to discuss your current price plan for your existing mobile phone. Leave a message if you can't get through (most likely it'll be because I'm in court).

I look forward to your swift and positive response!

Ever,

R*

* Presumably Richard? Odd to see Ayoade refer to himself using his Christian name.

A Letter from an Actor

Just finished your script. Sorry for the delay, but I couldn't read more than two pages at a time without becoming incredibly fatigued. It seemed remarkably similar to draft thirty, or am I imagining this because of the crippling depression I now feel?

Have you cut the scene where Tony teaches the raccoon to hang-glide? A shame, as that was one of the few moments I believed. The beginning still feels like an eternity. But perhaps that's what you want? Do you want the audience to be so bored they're grateful that *anything* happens? That could be interesting, but at the moment it's unclear. I'm still not sure whether this is a brave script or a terrible script. This may become more obvious when (if?) you shoot it. BTW, is it true that you're not really involved in the actual making of the film? That you just sit in a corner and rock back and forth? If not, and you are more of a presence on set, perhaps you could triangulate any questions via my acting trainer. He's amazing. He trains me AND acts. He also designs my celery cleanses. You should get into them, except they're secret so you can't. God, I'm hungry.

So, let's talk about the character. We need one. Unless the idea is that he's *meant* to be a non-person? Like a void or a nothing? Perhaps you'll manage to evoke a believable figure with the editing or the way you light it or something. Look, the point is I've given you my word for some reason so I probably won't back out (although my agent says I totally could back out – why do you think we haven't signed the contracts yet?).

283

Anyway, here are a few thoughts on this version.

p. 1 It says, 'Fade in. We see Tony showering.' Who's 'we'? This whole start feels like a conspiracy film: 'We follow him as he walks to his car'; 'We stay with him as he enters the office.' Why would 'They' want to watch him so closely? And why wouldn't Tony notice?

p. 3 Do you think the line 'I trained as a combat vet' might be confusing? We MUST be clear that he was a *veterinarian* in the army and not a *veteran* in the army. Also – does the army even have vets? Maybe the cavalry does? Do they still use horses in wars? Why can't we do something to stop this? I mean they're just horses – what did they ever do?

p. 12 Instead of 'I can't feel my hands any more,' Tony should say, 'My hands. My hands! Can't feel my hands!' Much more playable. This guy really can't feel his hands, and he's not about to hold back. That's what I'd say in real life if I couldn't feel *my* hands. Remember: film is emotion.

p. 25 Wouldn't he get even *more* upset at the way the animal drop-in center is being managed? I mean who *is* this new boss? The fact that she's a woman just seems to make things doubly infuriating.

pp. 28–90 Do we need pp. 28–90?

284

Big Julian: A Short Film by Ayoade

A stretch of icy road.

BIG JULIAN stands at the doorway of a HOUSE. He has a boyish haircut and is overweight. He rings the bell. The door opens. Behind it is a TINY BUTLER, about the height of a hen.

> BIG JULIAN
>
> I've come for my drink. The woman said I could come in for my drink.

The TINY BUTLER opens the door. The man walks into the house, removes his shoes and follows the tiny butler to the sitting room. In the sitting room are a MAN (HAROLD), a WOMAN and a VERY OLD MAN (WALTER). The woman stands up.

> TINY BUTLER
>
> There's a man here.

> WOMAN
>
> Hello. You made it then?

> BIG JULIAN
>
> Yes. For a while I thought I wouldn't.

HAROLD

Really?

BIG JULIAN

Yes. (*Beat.*) I really did think that. (*Beat.*) You don't
have to get me any food. I'm not hungry. I won't eat.
I couldn't *eat*.

WOMAN

Would you like something to drink?

BIG JULIAN

I'd like coffee. Coffee and whiskey.

*The WOMAN goes to the kitchen to make the drink. The
TINY BUTLER follows her. BIG JULIAN sits down in
an armchair. HAROLD is sitting on the sofa opposite.*

BIG JULIAN

It's good to be inside. On a day like this.

HAROLD

They say it's below zero.

BIG JULIAN

Do they?

HAROLD

That's what they say.

BIG JULIAN

I don't know your Christian name.

HAROLD

It's Harold.

BIG JULIAN

I like you, Harold. You say what you think.

There's a long pause. WALTER starts to make a strange snorting sound for a while.

Then he stops.

The WOMAN returns, now carrying the whiskey and coffee. She sets them down at a table in front of BIG JULIAN. BIG JULIAN takes quick gulps of the two drinks.

No one's smoking, are they? None of you here smoke, do you? I shouldn't smoke. I'm too big to smoke.

WOMAN

We don't smoke in this house.

BIG JULIAN
(*lighting his cigarette*)
Don't you? I should stop. Really. I mean to very soon. Ask your tiny butler for an ashtray. An ashtray. My tiny butler died, you see.

Pause.

Ashtray. (*Beat.*) Ashtray?

Walter goes to get up and fetch the ashtray.

Sit down. You're too old. *God.* Let the tiny butler get it. *You're far too old.*

The TINY BUTLER brings in a mug, before disappearing out into the kitchen.

This is a mug. You can't fool me. This is a mug. Is this a joke? This is a mug.

HAROLD

None of us smoke.

BIG JULIAN

Do you want a medal? Is that what you want? Do you want me to make you a medal while I tap ash into a mug? Fine, I'll do it.

He taps his ash into the mug.

Pause.

It's a quiet area, isn't it? It's quiet round here.

WOMAN

Yes. Very quiet.

HAROLD

We're quite lucky with the noise. We don't hear anything.

288

WOMAN

It's very quiet.

BIG JULIAN

And you don't hear me, do you?

HAROLD

No, no. No complaints.

BIG JULIAN

I keep myself to myself.

HAROLD

We've no complaints.

BIG JULIAN

I pay my rent . . .

HAROLD

Yes. Without fail.

BIG JULIAN

No slip-ups.

HAROLD

None that I've seen . . .

BIG JULIAN

You can't ask for more than that.

HAROLD

You've been a very conscientious tenant. We've no
complaints.

BIG JULIAN

I have a house that I go to in the summer. My grand-
mother gave it to me. It's small, but I can go there
and look at the sea. I have a photo of it downstairs.
Maybe one day I'll bring it round.

WOMAN

Where's that?

BIG JULIAN
(*ignoring her*)
I think it's on one of the walls.

WALTER *starts to make more strange sounds.*

It's a bit big for me now. As you get older, places
seem bigger. You shrink when you get older, don't
you?

WOMAN

My mother did.

BIG JULIAN

What did you say?

WOMAN

My mother shrank down to nothing.

BIG JULIAN

What did she say?

WOMAN

What?

BIG JULIAN

Did she say anything about her shrinking?

WOMAN

I don't think so.

BIG JULIAN

Just kept it to herself. Wouldn't be drawn. (*Beat.*) I have a picture of my tiny butler. But I probably left it next to the one of my house.

WOMAN

Maybe another time . . .

BIG JULIAN

I hope I didn't burn it. (*Beat.*) My tiny butler was killed just up by that road.

BIG JULIAN motions with his hand. We see the road that he's talking about. It is the road we saw previously.

WOMAN

I'm very sorry.

BIG JULIAN

You should keep an eye on your tiny butler. Because they're there one minute, and the next minute . . .

He clicks his fingers.

. . . they're gone.

WOMAN

What do you mean?

The phone rings.

BIG JULIAN

Well . . . that'll be me.

BIG JULIAN gets up to go.

WOMAN

What do you mean?

*BIG JULIAN leaves the house. The phone is still ring-
ing. HAROLD and the WOMAN look at the telephone.*

HAROLD

Who's that?

WOMAN

I don't know yet.

The WOMAN picks up the phone.

Hello? Yes, this is she . . .

HAROLD

Is he gone?

WALTER

Is who gone?

The WOMAN listens to a voice on the phone.

HAROLD

What is it?

WALTER

Is who gone?

HAROLD

The man.

HAROLD *turns back to the* WOMAN.

What is it?

WALTER

What man? There was no man.

The WOMAN *puts down the phone and stares out.*

HAROLD

What is it?

WOMAN

That was him.

Their eyes meet.

That was Big Julian.

HAROLD

Where's our tiny butler, woman?

He grabs her shoulders.

Where's our tiny butler?

Tableau.

Coda: BIG JULIAN turns to look at his wall. We see two pictures. One is of BIG JULIAN outside his summer house, and the other is of a TINY BUTLER. The TINY BUTLER in the picture looks the same as the TINY BUTLER who opened the door to BIG JULIAN. We start to travel down the road where BIG JULIAN said his TINY BUTLER was killed.

Slow fade.

Fin.

Star Wars Blu-Ray Preview

There are few more heart-warming stories than Disney's recent purchase of Lucasfilm for $4.05 billion. Disney's chief executive Bob Iger, whose naive romanticism is matched only by his unquenching thirst for the common weal, couldn't bridle his joy any longer: 'This transaction combines a world-class portfolio of content . . . across multiple platforms, businesses, and markets to generate sustained growth and drive significant long-term value.' Art, that rambunctious thimblerigger, will intoxicate the most steadfast of men. Herewith an exciting taste of some of the deleted scenes that may appear in the latest *Star Wars* QuadraQuartzBluBox re-release.

– Luke Skywalker and a Treadwell droid discuss the best way of harvesting excess atmospheric humidity.

– A shot of an instruction manual for a moisture vaporator.

– A closer detail of the above.

– Luke eats a sandwich and berates a (different) droid for not cutting off the crusts and then apologises, saying he's been feeling tense and that maybe it's the heat or something.

– Luke's Landspeeder races into the town of Anchorhead and nearly runs over an old man. Luke again apologises and says he's been upset all day and that maybe it's the heat or something, or possibly the fact that his goddamn droid didn't even have the decency to cut the crusts off his sandwich. They exchange insurance details.

– Luke talks to Biggs Darklighter, who's using his macro-binoculars to watch a purple woman take a shower. Biggs says she has a great rack. Luke says aren't they getting too old for this? Biggs says lighten up, and if she didn't want people to look, she should get thicker shower curtains. Luke says that it just makes him kind of sad is all.

– Luke does crunches by a sand dune.

– Uncle Owen and Luke search for a missing turbo-spanner. Uncle Owen says he can't find it anywhere. Luke says when did you last have it? Uncle Owen says that if he knew that he wouldn't need to look for it.

– Han Solo visits a shop to return the stereo system for the *Millennium Falcon*. He says that it sounds crackly and that it's pretty bad seeing as he's only had it a month. Chewbacca joins in the remonstration and becomes so impassioned that he knocks over some blue juice onto a music system, which begins to fizz and starts to play space jazz in a stop–start way. The shop owner rebukes Chewbacca for his clumsiness, the space jazz a comic counterpoint to his ire. Chewbacca growls and throws the shop owner across the room. The shop owner offers them a full refund or exchange.

– An alternate take of Luke on a space cruiser wearing a beret.

– An additional rebel pilot, known as Gordon, says he

296

won't get into his spacecraft unless someone can find his inhaler.

– Uncle Owen says he wishes he didn't have such bad wind, that he's been haunted by wind his whole life, and that one day Luke'll know the true humiliation and agony of wind. Luke says he sometimes gets wind, but that it rarely lasts long. Uncle Owen says sometimes he gets wind so bad he wishes he were dead.

Ayoade on Crowdsourcing

Whenever I encounter my several fans, be it in the doorway of my house or in the back seat of a jeep, they always scream the exact same thing: 'How can we help you live free from any financial pressure?' And when I suggest in all humility that they, mere bog-standard people with ordinary lives and ordinary faces filled with oven chips and pre-sliced white bread, might have greater financial woes than me, these inspirational commoners never fail to retort, 'Are you KIDDING? We know how hard it is to get funding for passion projects in television and film. Just let us know if we can do ANYTHING to help you stay true to your vision.'

So this appeal is for you, my loyal supporters throughout the globe. Please give me everything that you can.

Hey,
My name is Richard Ayoade and I'm one of the least-respected actors of my generation. A couple of years ago I bought a house. It's a fine house – not too big – and the area's okay. Not great. But fine. It's a little hard to get into town on public transport, but that's life. It's one of the reasons the area's still relatively affordable. I used to be near an underground station, and that was great. Tubes every few minutes. I'm on an overground now. If I miss a train and the next one's delayed I could be on the platform for over twenty minutes. Sometimes I get the bus, but it drives me crazy that

it has to stop all the time to let people on and off. But that's my cross, and I'm in charge of it: I've got a big back.

The point is, I have a mortgage. A really big and upsetting mortgage. And The Money Men insist that I repay it. Every month!

WITH INTEREST!!!!

I'd like to have the creative freedom to say, 'No. I don't want to pay The Money Men this month. Or any month for that matter. I need to dream of a story to tell. Or find someone else with a story to tell and buy it from them. And make that story into a film that shows for a short time in selected theatres.' How can I feel free to do whatever I want if I'm in debt to completely uncreative people who won't give me money without asking for it back at some stage? That's where you come in. I want to make YOU a part of MY debt.

Pledge $10 and get a PDF copy of my mortgage repayments thus far.

Pledge $25 and get a PDF copy of my upcoming utility bills.

Pledge $50 and you will be cc'd on any correspondence with my bank manager.

Pledge $100 and I will tell you how much money I actually owe (in an email).

Let's take this journey together.

(NB: Pledging money does not mean you own any part of my house. It does not mean we are friends, and I WILL be rude to you if you approach me in the street – even if you are with your so-called 'son'.)

Epilogu(e)nding:
An Adieu to Arms

Ayoade has dirt on his hands. His black suit is flecked with soil. He plunges a spade deep into an indifferent earth. The wind wraps itself round a leafless tree. Ayoade's grief engulfs him – his knees yield – he falls – all the way – to the floor. His hands grasp out for redemption; he finds fistfuls of sod.

Ayoade weeps.

Ayoade is at a funeral.

Ayoade is the only mourner.

In the coffin lies a single canister of film. Its contents? A single image, shot in VistaVision, of Ayoade's head spliced with the head of Martin Scorsese. One says, '*Fin*.' The other says, 'Cinema.'*

Both are right.

Each is true.

The year is 2020.

The world has forgotten meaning. The world has forgotten Cinema. The world has forgotten itself.

Because the world has forgotten Ayoade.

I don't want to live in that world. None of us do.

So let us never forget.

Let us never stop giving thanks.

---

* From the quality, it seems as though the footage was ripped directly from YouTube and then *transferred back* to film, meaning that the footage had, ironically, gone through a digital intermediate process (*op. cit.*). Inexplicable impurity? Or a metaphor for Ayoade himself: one foot in the past, one foot in Martin Scorsese?

Let us always remember just what it is that we *have*.

We have Ayoade.

We have Cinema.

We must hold both close to our hearts before the wind blows them away.

Ayoade on Ayoade would not have been possible without the kind assistance of Ayoade. It was edited down from over one thousand hours of audio recordings to a more manageable two hours. This was achieved by simply discarding all but two of the tapes. This book is a transcript of those two remaining tapes.

Index